Recycling Activities for the Primary Grades

by Jean Stangl

Fearon Teacher Aids
Simon & Schuster Education Group

723536

Editorial Director: Virginia L. Murphy

Editor: Carol Williams

Copyeditor: Kristin Eclov

Cover Design and Illustration: Teena Remer

Inside Illustration: Teena Remer

Design: Terry McGrath

Production: Rebecca Speakes

ISBN 0-86653-938-7

Printed in the United States of America

1. 9 8 7 6 5 4 3

Table of Contents

Introduction

Don't throw away those old newspapers, paper bags, boxes, or cartons. Recycle them into classroom activities, projects, and teaching tools. Discover how to make students aware of the importance of recycling, how to save on your materials budget, and new ways to provide learning experiences using "throw-aways."

Recycling Activities for the Primary Grades provides you with projects and activities for all areas of the curriculum using easy-to-collect recyclables. Creative movement activities will encourage children to move and learn using simple props they can make. Hands-on science tools and unusual math manipulatives will encourage children to be active participants in the learning process. "Throw-aways" will be transformed into unique art and craft projects. Language arts takes on a new meaning as reading skills are fostered through the use of newspaper headlines, paper bag logos, and box labels. Add interest to dramatic play with costumes, masks, and other fun-to-wear accessories.

Since storage space is often limited in many classrooms, don't try to collect all the materials at the same time. Decide on the projects and activities you want to include in your curriculum over a month's time. Send a note home to each family asking for their help in collecting the necessary recyclable materials.

As part of the learning experience, involve children in sorting and storing the materials. For example, children can help tie newspapers in bundles, flatten paper bags, and store smaller boxes inside larger ones.

Young children will take pride in being responsible for collecting, sorting, and storing their own learning materials and will be eager to display completed projects in the cafeteria or library. They might also like to give how-to demonstrations to other classes.

Recycling Activities for the Primary Grades will make it easy for you to integrate recycling activities and projects into every area of the curriculum as well as help your students learn to reuse, recycle, and rethink. So start making plans for collecting newspapers, paper bags, boxes, and cartons and bring a new dimension of recycling to your students as they discover the joy and satisfaction of creating "something new" from "something old."

Part 1

NEWSPAPERS

Encourage children to crush, tear, fold, staple, and cut newspapers into a myriad of creations, designs, and experiments as they create their own learning forum.

Chapter 1 Creative Movement with the Newspaper

Using newspapers for props will add interest to your movement and exercise program and will help lengthen the attention span of your young participants. The props are easy to make and require few materials.

Newspaper Wands

Wand Action

✔ Newspaper, adhesive-backed paper, rubber bands

Fold three sheets of newspaper in half twice. Starting at the long end, roll the newspaper tightly into a tube. Secure each end of the newspaper tube with a rubber band. Cover the tube with colored adhesive-backed paper. Make a wand for each child using different colors and patterns of paper. Invite young children to use wands to identify body parts, locations, colors, or numbers. For example, encourage children to touch the wand to their elbow, knee, or right ear. Invite children to tap their heads three times. Or, ask everyone who is holding a blue wand to hop four times.

Rhythm Wands

✔ Newspaper, adhesive-backed paper, rubber bands

Make two wands for each child as described in "Wand Action." Encourage children to use the wands as rhythm sticks by tapping them together to create sound patterns.

Wand Directions

✔ Newspaper, adhesive-backed paper, rubber bands

Make a red fringed wand and a blue fringed wand for each child. Cover only two-thirds of the wand with adhesive-backed paper. Fringe the uncovered portion by tearing each layer of newspaper into narrow strips. Invite each child to hold a red wand in one hand and a blue wand in the other. Give children directions for moving each wand and then both wands at the same time. Provide experiences in unilateral, bilateral, symmetrical, and asymmetrical movement. Include directions that require crossing the midline of the body with the wands.

Sports Play

Boat Rowing

✔ Newspaper, adhesive-backed paper, rubber bands

Make two wands for each child as described in "Wand Action." Invite children to use their wands as oars as they row a pretend boat while singing "Row, Row, Row Your Boat."

Hockey

✔ Newspaper, tape, large cardboard box

Tightly roll several sheets of newspaper to form a long wand. Secure the wand with tape. Make a wand for each child. Invite children to use the long wands as hockey sticks. Provide a large cardboard box (tipped on its side) to serve as a hockey goal.

Golf

✔ Newspaper, tape, newspaper balls, shoe boxes

Tightly roll several sheets of newspaper to form a long wand. Secure the roll with tape. Invite children to use the long wands as golf clubs by swinging at small newspaper balls. Arrange shoe boxes (tipped on their sides) in a golf course pattern.

Batting Practice

✔ Newspaper, masking tape, newspaper wands

Crush full sheets of newspaper into tight balls. Cover the balls with masking tape, shaping them as you wind strips of tape around the paper. Suggest that children use a newspaper wand for a bat. Invite children to work in pairs to practice batting the balls.

Newspaper Balls

Roll, Roll, Roll

✔ Newspaper, masking tape, box or wastebasket

Crush full sheets of newspaper into tight balls. Cover the balls with masking tape, shaping them as you wind strips of tape around the paper. Invite children to roll the newspaper balls. They can roll them back and forth to each other or roll them into the open end of a box or wastebasket.

Toss and Catch

✔ Newspaper, knee-high nylon stockings

Push a crushed newspaper ball into the toe of a nylon stocking. Twist the end of the stocking several times. Turn the inside of the stocking back over the newspaper ball to form a double stocking cover. Continue twisting and turning the stocking back over the ball until the stocking is completely used. Or, after covering the ball once with the stocking, leave the remaining portion of the stocking free to give the ball a "tail." (Younger children may be more successful at throwing and catching a ball with a tail.) Encourage children to toss the newspaper balls. Children can practice tossing the balls (from various distances) through hoops, through different-sized holes cut in a board, or into different-sized containers. Invite children to work in pairs to practice tossing and catching.

Color Code

✔ Newspaper, colored adhesive-backed paper

Crush full sheets of newspaper into tight balls. Cover the balls with colored adhesive-backed paper. Provide children with color identification practice. For example, ask children to toss the blue ball or roll the green ball towards the door.

Swinging Target

✔ Newspaper ball with a tail, heavy string, newspaper wand

Tie a piece of heavy string to a newspaper ball that already has a tail. Suspend the ball from the ceiling so it hangs at a child's chest level. Invite children to use a wand bat to hit the moving ball. This is a great activity to help develop eye-hand coordination and tracking.

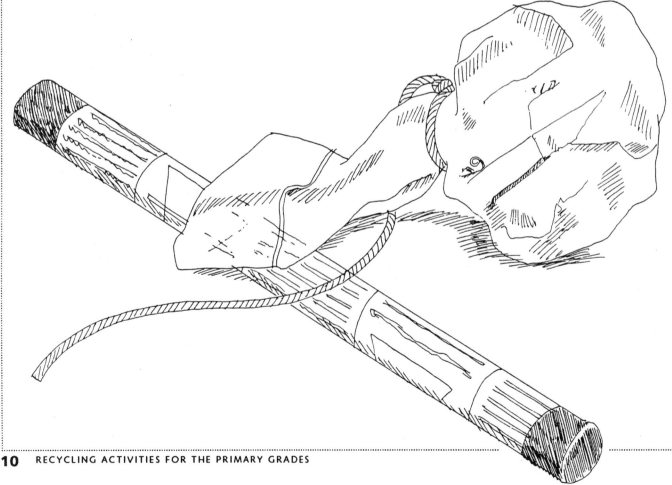

Tearing and Crushing Newspapers

Musical Tearing

✔ Newspaper, music

Encourage children to tear newspaper strips. Play music and invite children to tear slowly or quickly according to the tempo. Encourage children to tear long strips, short strips, wide strips, and narrow strips. This is a great small motor and eye-hand coordination activity. Save the strips in a box to use for another project later.

Newspaper Pond

✔ Newspaper, bed sheet

Spread torn and shredded newspaper on a bed sheet. Invite children to walk on the sheet with their bare feet and then roll in, sit in, or cover their legs with the newspaper strips. Save the paper for stuffing or a future papier-mâché project.

Hat Balance

✔ Newspaper

Invite each child to tear a 4" square of newspaper and wear it on his or her head as a magic elf hat. Challenge children to tiptoe to the story rug, hop to the door, or jump backwards across the room while keeping their "hats" on their heads. Challenge children to fold their arms across their chests, cross their legs, and sit down while keeping their hats in place. Children can place their hands on their hips and squat and rise slowly three times.

Right, Left Squeeze

✔ Newspaper

Invite children to hold both hands in front of them with their palms up. Place a half sheet of newspaper on top of each palm. Have children squeeze and crush the paper with their right hands and then open their hands to reveal a newspaper ball. Have children squeeze and crush with their left hands and open their hands to reveal another newspaper ball. Challenge children to squeeze with alternate hands or with both hands at once.

Right, Left Flick

✔ Newspaper, music

Invite each child to tear a 4" newspaper square and then tear the square in half. Invite children to crush each half into a tiny tight ball. Have children place the two balls on the floor in front of them. Challenge children to flick the right ball with their right hands and then the left ball with their left hands. This is fun to do to music. Children might also enjoy trying to pick up the tiny newspaper balls with their bare toes.

Newspaper Streamers

Streamer Twirl

✔ Newspaper, scissors, tape

Cut two 2"-wide strips the length of a newspaper page for each child. Tape the two strips end to end. Fold down one end to make a loop and tape in place for a handle. Invite children to twirl the streamers over their heads, around in circles, or behind them. Encourage children to twirl the streamers fast, slow, high, and low. Challenge children to suggest other ways to twirl their streamers, too.

Streamer Jumping

✔ Newspaper streamers

Invite children to form their streamers into circles. Encourage children to jump in and out of their circles. Begin jumping slowly and then challenge children to jump faster. Children can also place the streamers on the floor in front of them in a straight line and jump over them, hop around them, or tiptoe on them.

Streamer Creativity

✔ Newspaper streamers, music

Invite children to move to music with their streamers in creative ways. For integrating both sides of the body, encourage children to use a streamer in each hand. Suggest ideas for moving the streamers.

Newspaper Obstacle Courses

Musical Course

✔ Newspaper, scissors, tape, music

Invite children to help you set up an obstacle course in the classroom or play area using newspaper shapes and pictures. Cut "puddles" and "islands" from sheets of newspaper. Lay out pages with large pictures of fruits, vegetables, letters, numerals, and toys. Crush mounds of newspapers to make rocks, hills, and mountains. Lay out comic strips. Tape two or three newspaper pages end to end to make a pathway. Tape rolls of newspapers together to make a bridge. Tear strips of newspaper to make a pile of "leaves." Once the course is made, invite children to walk through the course to become familiar with it. Then play music as children maneuver through the obstacle course. Encourage children to move slowly when the music is slow and to move quickly when the music speeds up. Direct children to stand still when the music stops.

Course Directions

✔ Obstacle course

Give specific directions for moving through the "Musical Course" from the previous activity. Challenge children to jump over the rock, hop around the mountain, tiptoe down the trail, or take a giant step over the puddle. Or, direct children to stand on a picture of fruit or hop from a toy picture to a fruit picture to a comic strip.

Chapter 2 # Language Arts with the Newspaper

• •

Studying newspapers and discovering how they are written and put together can play a major role in your language arts program. Encourage students to become reporters, copyeditors, and designers as they put together their own classroom newspaper.

Discovering Newspapers

Newspaper Tour

✔ Newspapers

Ask your local newspaper publisher for enough copies of yesterday's newspaper for each student in your class to have a copy. Provide enough time for students to browse through their copies. Challenge children to locate the date, index, headlines, editorials, letters to the editor, comics, sport section, classified ads, and other sections of interest to your class.

Newspaper Hunt

✔ Newspapers, scissors, construction paper, glue

Invite children to locate, clip, and paste newspaper findings. Challenge younger students to find:

• ten things they have in their houses

• headline letters to spell their names

• large-sized numerals from 1 to 10

• the item and price of something that costs less than one dollar, more than five dollars, more than nineteen dollars, and so on

• all the letters of the alphabet

• three different sizes of the letter "A" and the numeral "5"

Challenge older students to find:

• ten appliances that operate with electricity

• words that are examples of a long vowel and a short vowel sound for each of the five vowels

• a word that begins with each letter of the alphabet

• five words that describe size

For Sale

✔ Newspapers, construction paper, scissors, glue

Invite children to look in the classified pages to locate two automobiles for sale. Have children cut out both and glue them opposite each other on a sheet of construction paper. Encourage children to compare the similarities and differences between the two cars. Challenge children to do the same for other items that are for sale as well.

Front Page

✔ Newspapers, scissors

Invite each child to cut out an article from the newspaper that they think is the most important news event of the day. Encourage children to share their articles with the class and discuss why they think the articles are important, as well as where they found them in the newspaper.

Scavenger Hunt

✔ Newspapers, scissors, construction paper, glue

Give each child a newspaper and a scavenger list. Challenge children to search the newspaper to find and cut out all items on their lists. A typical list might include:

picture of a breakfast cereal

price of a car

household hint

yesterday's high temperature

publisher of the newspaper

author of an advice column

a photographer's name

Word Builder

✔ Newspapers, lined paper, pencils, dictionary

Invite children to search through the newspaper and find five unfamiliar words. Have children list the words on a sheet of paper. Encourage children to look up the words in a dictionary and write a definition for each one. Compile a classroom list and use the new words for vocabulary practice or for spelling words.

WORDS
expansive
scavenger
encourage
construction
price
merchandise
personalities

Letters and Words

Alphabet Collage

✔ Newspaper, scissors, construction paper, glue

Invite children to cut letters from the newspaper and glue them to a sheet of construction paper to create an alphabet collage. (Children could also make a number collage in the same way.)

Circle It

✔ Newspaper, felt markers

Challenge children to find and circle all the letter A's they can find in a given paragraph. Or, encourage children to circle dollar signs, numbers, three-letter words, and so on. Invite children to use a different color of felt marker for each search.

Smallest to Largest

✔ Newspaper, scissors, construction paper, glue

Invite children to cut five different-sized pictures of the same object from the newspaper. For example, children could cut out five pictures of a car or five pictures of a person. Challenge children to glue the pictures on a sheet of construction paper from smallest to largest.

Alphabet Books

✔ Newspaper, drawing paper, scissors, glue, stapler

Have each child staple 26 half sheets of drawing paper together to make a book. Invite children to cut a large letter from the newspaper for each letter of the alphabet. Encourage students to glue one letter on each page of their books in alphabetical order. Challenge children to find a word or picture that begins with each letter to add to the pages. Children can glue several pictures to each page and then label the pictures to turn their books into picture dictionaries.

Creative Writing

Greeting Cards

✔ Newspaper, scissors, glue, construction paper, pencils

Invite children to cut a picture from the newspaper and glue it to the front of a folded piece of construction paper. Encourage children to write a greeting or verse inside their cards.

News Headlines

✔ Newspaper, scissors, glue, lined paper, pencils

Encourage children to cut a picture of an inanimate object from the newspaper. Have children glue the picture to a sheet of lined paper and write a short news story from the point of view of the object.

Creating Ads

✔ Newspaper, scissors, glue, lined paper, pencils

Invite children to cut out a picture of an item in the newspaper that is for sale. Have children glue the picture on a sheet of lined paper. Challenge children to write a sales pitch from the item's point of view.

Lost and Found

✔ Newspaper, scissors, glue, lined paper, pencils

Invite children to study the "Lost and Found" section of the newspaper and notice the style of descriptive writing used. Encourage children to cut a picture from the newspaper and glue it to a sheet of lined paper. Challenge students to write a "lost" or "found" ad describing the article.

Comic Strips

✔ Newspaper, scissors, glue, drawing paper, pencils

Have each child select a comic strip from the newspaper and cut it out. Invite children to cut off the dialogue and glue only the pictures, in their proper sequence, on a sheet of drawing paper. Students can exchange papers with a classmate and create appropriate dialogue to accompany the comic pictures.

Creative Comics

✔ Newspaper, scissors, envelopes, box, glue, drawing paper

Have each child select a comic strip from the newspaper and cut it out. Invite children to cut around each character and place all the characters in an envelope. Have all students place their envelopes in a box. Invite each student to choose one envelope from the box, remove the pieces, and arrange the characters as desired on a sheet of paper. Students can glue the characters in place. Encourage students to give their comic strips names and write dialogue for each character.

Newspaper Carrier

✔ Lined paper, pencils

Discuss the job of a newspaper carrier. Encourage students to write a short story entitled "A Day in the Life of a Newspaper Carrier."

Letters to the Editor

✔ Newspaper, lined paper, pencils

Study and discuss letters written to the editor. Encourage students to write a letter to the editor expressing their views on a community matter. You may want to consider compiling a classroom letter to the editor and actually mailing it.

Classroom Newspaper

✔ Newspaper, lined paper, blank newsprint, dictionaries, pencils, scissors, crayons, felt markers, glue

If possible, arrange for your class to visit a newspaper office or have a staff person speak to the class. After studying and discussing the format of newspapers, make a list of necessary tasks involved in producing a small newspaper. Invite each student to be a "reporter" and write a news article for your classroom newspaper. When all the articles are submitted, assign jobs, set deadlines, decide on size and format, choose a name for your newspaper, and so on. Discuss the importance of proofreading and rewriting. Discuss the aesthetic quality of a newspaper that is determined by such factors as headline style, pictures, and layout design. Calculate how many copies of your classroom newspaper you will need to print. If you decide to charge a small fee for the newspaper, keep a ledger of expenses and income. When the contents are completed satisfactorily, print your newspaper.

Chapter 3 # Science with the Newspaper

· ·

Use newspapers in your science center for a variety of experiments. Give students opportunities to explore, make predictions, and test their ideas.

Exploring Newspapers

Close-Up Print

✔ Newspaper, magnifying glasses

Invite students to use magnifying glasses to examine the newspaper print up close. Encourage children to share what they discover.

Picture Perfect

✔ Newspaper, magnifying glasses

Encourage children to examine a newspaper photograph using a magnifying glass. The hand lens will enable children to see that the photograph is made up of numerous tiny black dots.

Absorption and Evaporation

Predicting Absorption

✔ Newspaper, clear plastic cups, water, measuring cup

Invite each child to crush a half sheet of newspaper and place it in a cup. Have children predict how much water the crushed newspaper will absorb. Have children measure a cup of water and slowly pour it over the crushed newspaper. Instruct children to stop pouring water when the newspaper is saturated. Challenge children to calculate how much of the cup of water they poured and to compare the results to their original prediction.

Paper Dip

✔ Newspaper, construction paper, butcher paper, typing paper, tub of water

Invite children to work in groups to compare absorption and evaporation of water on various types of paper. Have children dip a sheet of newspaper, construction paper, butcher paper, and typing paper in a tub of water. Instruct children to carefully remove the paper from the water and lay the sheets out on the sidewalk in the hot sun. Encourage children to observe what happens to the paper. Challenge children to consider what this experiment tells them about different types of paper.

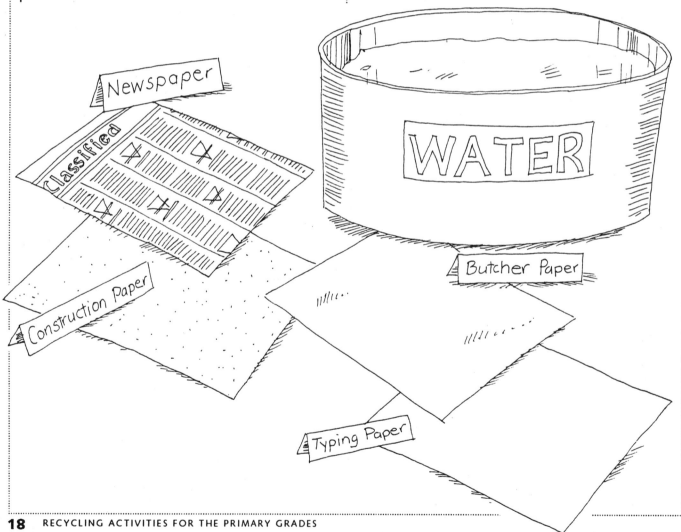

Newspaper Gardening

Sprouting Seeds

✔ Newspaper, bowls, water, seeds
(lima bean, alfalfa, cress)

Invite children to work in groups. Have each group fold a sheet of newspaper to fit the bottom of a bowl. Have children pour water on the paper until it is saturated and place several seeds on the wet paper. Encourage children to place the bowls on a windowsill or shelf away from direct sun. Children will need to keep the paper wet over the next few days. When green shoots appear, have children place the bowls in the sun. Continue to keep the paper wet and the plants will grow for several weeks.

Potting Mulch

✔ Newspaper, dictionary, pots,
potting soil, lima bean seeds, scissors

Invite children to look up the word *mulch* in the dictionary. Discuss the importance of using mulch for plants. Invite each group of three or four students to fill a pot two-thirds full with potting soil. Have children mix a tablespoon of finely shredded newspaper into the soil. Encourage students to punch holes about 1/2" deep into the soil mix and drop a lima bean seed in each hole. Instruct students to cover each seed with soil and cover the soil with a thin layer of finely shredded newspaper. Water well and place the pots in the sun. Keep the mulch damp and the bean shoots should appear in about four or five days.

School Yard Mulch

✔ Newspaper, scissors

Newspaper makes great organic mulch because it is seventy-five percent ground wood pulp and twenty-five percent purified fiber or cellulose. It contains all the nutrients and trace elements found in trees from which the paper was made. Invite students to cut or tear newspaper into narrow strips to make a paper mulch for the shrubs and plants around the school yard. Be sure to water the mulch well. Over a period of time, students can observe firsthand how newspapers act as a mulch and return nutrients to the soil. When the newspaper decomposes, it can be tilled back into the soil.

Newspaper Music

Tube Sounds

✔ Newspaper, rubber bands

Have children roll newspapers into different-sized tubes. Encourage students to roll some tightly and others loosely. Invite children to tap the tubes on a table to find out what sound each makes. Challenge students to create a "song" or sound pattern with the tubes.

Newspaper Sounds

✔ Newspaper

Invite children to experiment rolling sheets of newspaper into shapes of different sizes and lengths. Encourage students to find ways to make sounds with the shapes by blowing into them, tapping them, or by creating another method.

Newspaper Nutrition

Food Pyramid

✔ Newspaper grocery ads, scissors, glue, posterboard

Invite children to cut food pictures from newspaper grocery ads. Encourage students to choose foods from each section of the food pyramid. Have children glue the pictures to posterboard to create food collages.

Balanced Meals

✔ Newspaper grocery ads, scissors, paper plates, glue

Encourage each child to cut food pictures from the newspaper grocery ads that would be appropriate for a balanced meal. Invite children to glue their meals on a paper plate.

Place Mats

✔ Newspaper grocery ads, waxed paper, brushes, glue, scissors

Give each child a sheet of waxed paper appropriately sized for a place mat. Invite children to cut food pictures from the newspaper grocery ads and arrange them on the waxed paper. Have children brush glue over the waxed paper and the food pictures. Give each child a second sheet of waxed paper of equal size to place on top. When dry, children can trim the edges of the paper place mat or cut it into a shape of their choice.

Healthy Snacks

✔ Newspaper grocery ads, scissors

Invite children to cut out pictures of snack foods from the newspaper grocery ads. Encourage children to notice how many of the foods are healthy snacks and how many are considered "junk food." Make a class graph on the chalkboard to show the results.

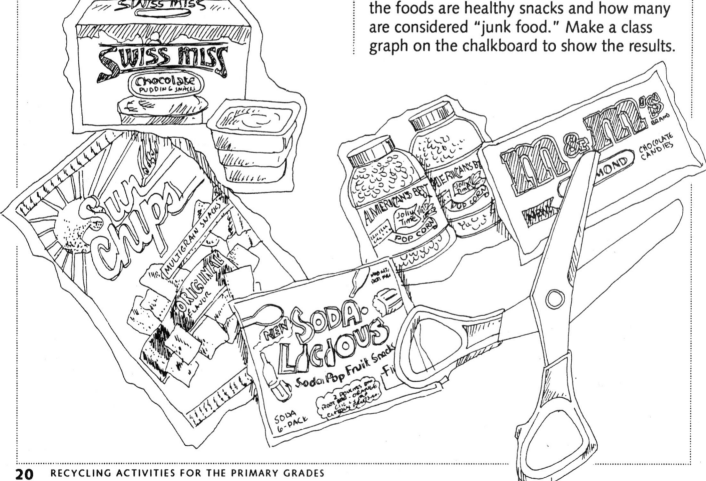

Chapter 4 **Math with the Newspaper**

As your newspaper collection continues to grow, invite students to hone their math skills by calculating height, weight, and cost of the paper stacks.

Collecting

Planning Ahead

✔ Telephone book

Discuss with students how recycled newspapers can be used. Ask students to bring in samples of recycled paper items. Invite students to check the telephone Yellow Pages to find the closest recycling center. Call and check the hours of operation and the current rate for recycled newspapers. Discuss with children how to collect the papers, where they will be stored, who will deliver them to the recycling center, and how the class will spend the profits. If possible, arrange for the entire class to visit the recycling center for a field trip, or invite an employee of the recycling center to come speak to the class. Set a deadline for the collection project.

Newspaper Stacks

✔ Newspaper, string, felt markers, scale, tape measure

Invite each child to collect a stack of newspapers equal to his or her height or weight. Tie papers securely into bundles that are easy to carry. Encourage students to write their names across the tops of their bundles with a felt marker. Students could also create personalized signs, posters, or slogans to identify their stacks. Take the bundles to a recycling center.

In school we learned to recycle today —

Help save the world in one small way!

Look for Paul he's 40" tall!

Collection Ledger

✔ Newspaper collection, paper, pencils, tape measure, scale

Invite students to record significant data in a ledger as it relates to the collection of the newspaper stacks. Students might note the date papers were brought to class, the height of the stacks, the weight of the stacks, and the name of the contributor.

Graph It

✔ Newspaper collection, scale, notepaper, pencils

Invite children to collect newspapers for five days. Weigh and record the amount collected each day. Make a graph to show the results. Ask children what day the most newspapers were collected, what day the least were collected, and how much was collected altogether.

Add It Up

✔ Newspaper collection

Encourage children to find out the daily purchase price of a single newspaper. Challenge students to compute the total original price of their newspaper collection.

Measuring

How Tall Are You?

✔ Newspaper, scissors, tape

Invite children to cut strips of newspaper and tape them together to equal their height.

How Long Is Our Classroom?

✔ Newspaper, scissors, tape

Invite children to work in small groups to cut and tape newspaper strips together to equal the length (size) of the classroom.

Roll It Up

✔ Newspaper, scissors, tape

Invite children to work together in small cooperative groups. Challenge each group to cut strips of newspaper, tape the strips together, and roll the long strip into a roll. At the end of a predetermined time limit, see which group has the largest roll. Encourage older students to tally the number of strips used and calculate the length of the entire roll based on the length of one strip.

Paper Stretching

Spiral

✔ Newspaper, scissors, tape measure

Have students measure the longest length of an open sheet of newspaper. Then, have students cut the largest circle possible from the newspaper by rounding the corners. Encourage children to start cutting around the circumference of the circle about 1" from the edge. Have students continue cutting around and around until they reach the center to make one long spiral. Invite students to gently stretch the spiral and measure its length. Challenge students to consider which measurement (the length of the paper before cutting or the spiral) is longest and why.

Cornstalk

✔ Newspaper, tape, scissors

Invite each child to roll a half sheet of newspaper into a tube. Before rolling the last five inches, have children place another sheet to overlap the rolled sheet and continue rolling to within five inches. Have students continue adding paper until they have rolled six sheets together. Tape the edges in place. Invite children to cut four 4" slits down from the top of one end. Encourage children to hold the bottom of the tube with one hand and reach the other hand into the center and gently pull the center sheet upward. As children gently pull, the cornstalk will grow.

Puzzlers

How Many?

✔ Notepaper, pencils

Yolanda had two more stacks of newspapers than Jennifer.

Jennifer had one less stack of newspapers than Maria and only half as many as Victoria.

Maria had one less stack than Yolanda.

Victoria had two stacks containing 40 newspapers, three stacks containing 20 newspapers, and 7 stacks each with different amounts of newspapers.

How many stacks of newspapers did each girl have?

(Answer: Yolanda 8, Jennifer 6, Maria 7, Victoria 12.)

Chapter 5 **Art with the Newspaper**

The uses for newspaper in creative art and craft projects is limited only by one's imagination. Always keep an assortment of newspapers in the art center to challenge young children's creativity.

Newspaper Rolls

Wreath

✔ Newspaper, tape, glue, paint

Starting with the long edge, invite each child to loosely roll a double sheet of newspaper. Have students tape the roll in place. Invite students to bend the roll into a circle and then tape the two ends together. Students can tape a newspaper bow to the top of their wreaths. Invite children to use wet newspaper to form assorted sizes of newspaper balls. After the balls are dry, children can glue them to the wreath. Encourage children to paint their wreaths as well.

Sculptures

✔ Newspaper, tape, glue, cardboard

Invite children to roll newspapers, from corner to corner, into different-sized rolls. Secure the rolls with tape. Challenge students to create sculptures by bending and connecting the rolls. Children can glue their sculptures, either flat or upright, to a piece of cardboard.

Stick Puppets

✔ Newspaper, tape, scissors, glue, posterboard

Invite children to roll newspaper into a tight roll and tape in place. Have children cut a picture of a toy (doll, teddy bear, animal) from a newspaper ad. Children can glue the picture to a piece of posterboard and then to the top of the roll to make a stick puppet.

Building Logs

✔ Newspaper, tape, shellac spray

Invite children to make building logs by tightly rolling newspaper to form equal-size logs. Spray the rolled logs with shellac and allow them to dry and harden. Encourage children to use the logs to construct buildings, fences, and other structures.

Castles

✔ Newspaper, tape, glue, heavy cardboard, scissors, toothpicks, felt markers

Invite children to roll newspaper into different-sized rolls, varying the diameters and lengths. Secure the rolls with tape. Encourage students to construct castles by gluing or taping the rolls in an upright position on a piece of heavy cardboard. Have children fringe the top of the rolls, add newspaper cones, or newspaper flags taped to toothpicks. Children can draw windows and doors using felt markers.

Bulletin Boards

✔ Newspaper, stapler, pins, bulletin board

Invite children to make newspaper rolls to contribute to a class bulletin board. Pin or staple the rolls to the bulletin board in the shape of a tree, house, Jack-o'-lantern, or other shapes students suggest.

Picture Frame

✔ Newspaper, glue

Invite children to frame some of their favorite artwork by gluing thin, tightly rolled newspaper logs around a painting or drawing.

Pencil Holder

✔ Newspaper, pencils, tape, juice cans, glue

Have children roll a newspaper sheet around a pencil. Once the roll is secured with tape, have children slip the pencil out. Invite children to make enough rolls to cover a clean juice can. Encourage children to glue the rolls vertically to the outside of the can to completely cover it. Measure and cut the rolls to fit the height of the can.

Newspaper Stuffing

Beanbags

✔ Newspaper, scissors, stapler, paint, felt markers

Using three or four thicknesses of newspaper, invite children to cut two identical geometric shapes. Staple the two figures together, leaving an open space for stuffing. Have children tear newspaper into small shreds and stuff the shape. Staple the opening closed. Encourage children to use paint or felt markers to decorate the geometric-shaped beanbags.

Paper Pillows

✔ Newspaper, stapler, scissors, felt markers, paint

Invite each child to make a stuffed newspaper pillow. Cut, staple, and stuff pillows as described under "Beanbags." Encourage children to decorate their pillows in creative ways using felt markers and paint.

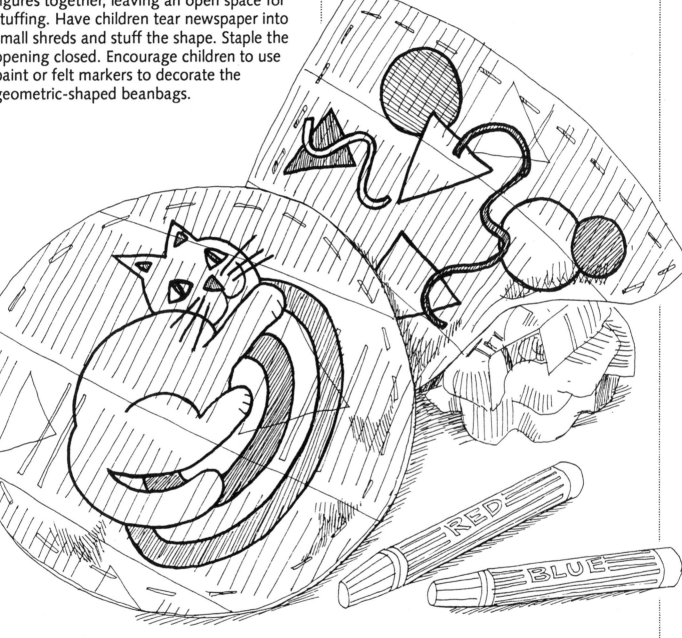

Paper People Puppets

✔ Newspaper, scissors, stapler,
felt markers, glue, yarn, ribbons,
tape

Invite each child to cut, staple, and stuff a 4" x 6" rectangle as described under "Beanbags." Encourage children to add facial features to the rectangle using felt markers. Children can glue on yarn hair, ribbons, and anything else they need to complete their puppets' heads. Invite children to fold strips of newspaper and staple in place for arms and legs. Encourage children to glue or staple their puppet bodies to a rolled tube of newspaper to make a handle.

Valentines

✔ Newspaper, scissors, stapler, red paint,
doilies, lace, ribbon, yarn, glue

Invite each child to cut two heart shapes from newspaper. Have children staple and stuff as described under "Beanbags." Encourage children to decorate their stuffed hearts as valentines using red paint, doilies, lace, and ribbon. Staple a loop of yarn to the top of each heart so it can be hung. Children can add arms and legs to their hearts by accordion-pleating strips of colorful glossy newspaper and stapling in place.

Mobiles

✔ Newspaper, tape, scissors,
hole punch, thread, yarn

Invite children to cut pictures of animals, clothing, people, or toys from glossy newspapers. Have children punch a hole in the top of each picture and tie different lengths of thread through each one. Encourage children to tie the free ends of the thread to a tightly rolled newspaper tube. Tie a loop of yarn in the center of the tube to hang the mobile.

Snowperson

✔ Newspaper, tape, white paint,
glue

Invite children to work in cooperative groups to make a snowperson. Have each group make a small, medium, and large pile of crushed newspaper. Instruct groups to wrap and tape double thicknesses of newspaper sheets around each pile, molding the piles into marshmallow shapes. Encourage children to stack the marshmallow shapes (largest on bottom and smallest on top) and secure with heavy tape. Children can paint the snowperson white. When dry, invite children to decorate with facial features and a hat cut from newspaper.

Octopus

✔ Newspaper, scissors, stapler,
pencils

Invite each child to cut, staple, and stuff two large newspaper circles as described in "Beanbags." Have children cut eight strips of newspaper and staple to the stuffed body to make octopus arms. Invite children to roll the ends of the arms tightly around a pencil to curl them. Children can use the same method to make stuffed spiders, ladybugs, or fish. Legs can be accordion-folded rather than curled.

Gift Wrapping

Package Wrap

✔ Newspaper, tape, scissors,
glue, felt markers

At holiday time, save colorful advertisement pages of the newspaper. Invite children to use the newspaper pages to wrap packages. Children can choose the paper that best matches the gift or suits the recipient. Children can also use the classified pages to wrap packages. Encourage children to use felt markers to decorate the wrapping or glue pictures cut from glossy sections of the newspaper.

Special Touches

✔ Newspaper, scissors, glue, tape

Encourage children to creatively decorate the top of their wrapped packages. Children can form long strips of colorful newspaper into designs on the top of the packages. Challenge children to make a bow or form the recipient's initials on a package top using newspaper strips. Children can cut a necktie, gingerbread person, football, or other appropriate shapes from colorful newspaper and glue them to the package top. Demonstrate how to roll 1" strips of newspaper to form rosettes, wheels, or candy designs. Children can try curling 1/4" wide strips by rolling them tightly around a pencil. Encourage children to try making interlocking chain loops to decorate their packages as well.

Gift Tubes

✔ Newspaper, stapler, yarn or ribbon, scissors

Encourage children to roll a sheet of newspaper into a tube with a large diameter. Have children fold and staple one end securely shut. Have children fringe the open end and then fill the tube with candy or a small gift. Invite children to tie the open end closed with yarn or ribbon.

Newspaper Designs

Night Scenes

✔ Newspaper, scissors, black construction paper, glue

Encourage children to cut shapes, such as trees, animals, roads, houses, boats, or a moon, from newspaper. Invite children to glue the shapes on a sheet of black construction paper to make a night scene.

Buildings

✔ Newspaper, scissors, white construction paper, glue

Invite children to cut or tear building shapes, such as houses, skyscrapers, or stores, from the colored pages of a newspaper. Have children glue the building shapes to a sheet of white construction paper.

Outline Designs

✔ Newspaper, glue, black construction paper, pencils

Have children draw the outline of a figure, such as a boat, flower, or house, on a sheet of black construction paper. Invite each child to outline the design with glue. Encourage children to roll tiny bits of newspaper into balls and press them on the wet glue outline.

Confetti Art

✔ Newspaper, pencils, white construction paper, glue, hole punch, scissors

Invite each child to draw a large outline of a simple object, such as an apple, pumpkin, or bell, on a sheet of white construction paper. Have children apply a thin layer of glue inside the design. Children can use a hole punch to make confetti from colored newspaper. Invite children to sprinkle the colorful confetti onto the wet glue.

Carbon Prints

✔ Newspaper, white paper, pencils

Have children choose a newspaper picture and place it over a sheet of white paper. Invite children to trace the outline of the picture while pressing firmly with their pencils. An outline of the picture will be duplicated on the white paper below.

Collages

✔ Newspaper, scissors, glue, construction paper

Children can cut or tear shapes from colored newspaper. Invite children to glue the shapes on a sheet of construction paper. Older children can cut characters from the comics or advertisement pages and glue them to a sheet of paper.

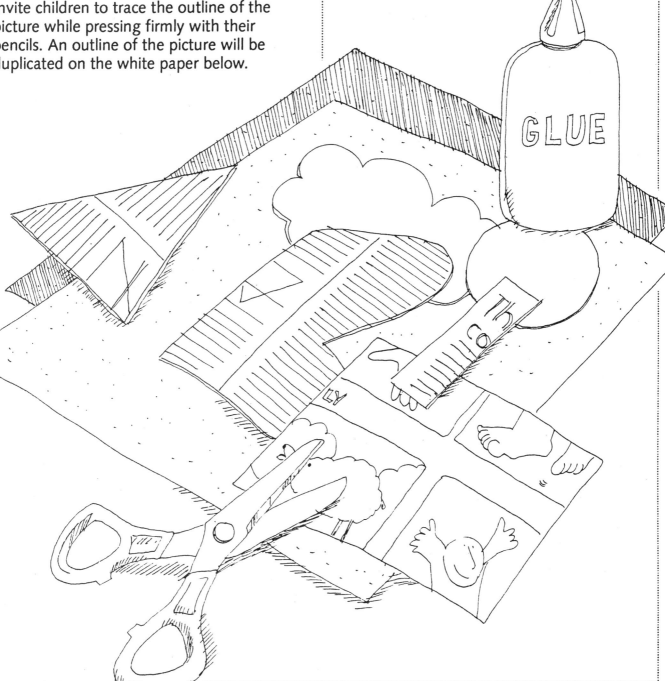

Ice-Cream Cone

✔ Newspaper, scissors, glue, construction paper

Invite children to cut a triangle shape from black and white newspaper to represent an ice-cream cone. Invite children to cut a circle from a colorful newspaper page to represent their favorite ice-cream flavor. Have children glue their cones and ice cream to a sheet of construction paper.

Classified Art

✔ Newspaper, black crayons, yellow paint

Give each student a sheet of newspaper from the classified section. Invite children to draw a picture on the newspaper using black crayon. When the drawing is complete, children can paint over it with yellow paint to create a crayon-resist design.

Folding Fun

Envelopes

✔ Newspaper, staple, glue

Challenge students to fold, staple, and glue sheets of newspaper to create envelopes.

Symmetrical Shapes

✔ Newspaper, scissors, pencils

Invite children to cut 5" newspaper squares. Encourage children to fold the squares in half and cut a symmetrical design, such as a heart, bell, or diamond, on the fold.

Fan

✔ Newspaper, scissors, stapler, hole punch, yarn

Invite children to cut an 8" x 15" sheet from glossy newspaper. Have children accordion-pleat the rectangle, starting at a short side. After the paper is completely pleated, staple through the folds at one end. Have children fan out the pleats. Punch a hole below the staple. Have children cut several 6" pieces of yarn and fold the bundle of yarn pieces in half. Have children insert the folded end through the hole punched in the end of the fan. Have children slip the free ends through the loop and pull tightly to make a tassel.

May Baskets

✔ Newspaper, scissors, glue, construction paper, pipe cleaners

Have each child cut an 8" square from a folded sheet of glossy newspaper. Invite children to fold two opposite corners to the center to form a cone. Have children overlap the corners and glue them together. Children can cut three 3" squares from colorful construction paper. Encourage children to pinch each square in the center and twist a pipe cleaner around it to make a flower. Invite children to place the flowers in their baskets.

Flowers

Lei

✔ Colorful newspaper, scissors, hole punch, yarn

Invite children to cut 2" squares from colorful sheets of newspaper. Have children accordion-pleat each square and punch a hole through the center. Children can thread the colorful "flowers" onto a piece of yarn. Tie the ends of the yarn together to make a necklace.

Stemmed Flowers

✔ Newspaper, stapler, pipe cleaners, scissors

Invite children to cut 2" squares from colorful sheets of newspaper. Have children accordion-pleat each square and staple through the center of the folds. Encourage children to experiment with different flower designs by fanning out the pleats, stacking one on top of the other, or fringing the ends of the paper. Have children twist a pipe cleaner around the center of each flower to make a stem.

Papier-Mâché

Puppets

✔ Newspaper, glue or liquid starch, plastic tubs, cardboard tubes (toilet tissue or paper towel), stapler, paint

Have each child crush a sheet of newspaper into a round ball to make a puppet head. Invite children to cover the head with two or three layers of newspaper strips that have been soaked in a mixture of equal parts of liquid starch and water or in a mixture of 1/4 cup glue added to a gallon of water. Before adding the last layer, encourage children to set the head on top of a cardboard tube. Add soaked newspaper strips to hold the head in place. When completely dry, invite children to paint the puppet heads and then cut clothing from newspaper to attach to the cardboard tube body.

Vases

✔ Newspaper, cans or plastic jars, glue or liquid starch, plastic tubs, paint

Invite children to cover a can or plastic jar with two or three layers of newspaper strips soaked in a mixture of equal parts of liquid starch and water or in a mixture of 1/4 cup glue added to a gallon of water. When completely dry, encourage children to paint their vases.

Newsprint

✔ Newspaper, glue or liquid starch, plastic tubs, waxed paper, rolling pin, pencils

Soak newspaper strips in a mixture of equal parts of liquid starch and water or in a mixture of 1/4 cup glue added to a gallon of water. Squeeze the excess liquid from a double handful of wet pulp. Place the pulp between two sheets of waxed paper. Invite children to use a rolling pin to press down on the waxed paper, rolling it as thin as possible. Let dry thoroughly. Invite children to try writing on the homemade paper.

Sculptures

✔ Newspaper, glue or liquid starch, plastic tubs, waxed paper, paint or felt markers

Soak newspaper strips in a mixture of equal parts of liquid starch and water or in a mixture of 1/4 cup glue added to a gallon of water. Invite each child to take a handful of the pulp and squeeze out the excess liquid. Have children place their handful of pulp on a sheet of waxed paper. Challenge children to form the pulp into a sculpture, such as a doll, clown, animal, or boat. When the sculptures are dry, children can paint them or add details with felt markers.

Chapter 6 # Dramatic Play with the Newspaper

Costumes, masks, hats, and accessories inspire children to enter the world of make-believe and creative play. Invite children to use props as they create imaginary fun.

Costumes

Pleated Skirt

✔ Newspaper, tape, stapler, large paper clips

Invite each student to fold a sheet of newspaper four times to make a 2"-wide band that is long enough to fit around his or her waist and overlap one inch. Invite children to make a skirt to attach to the waistband by taping double sheets of colorful newspaper end to end. Children can fold accordion-pleats along the width of the newspaper. Staple the pleated skirt between the folds of the waistband. Students can fasten the skirts around their waists with a large paper clip.

Hula Skirt

✔ Newspaper, tape, scissors, large paper clips

Invite each student to fold a sheet of newspaper four times to make a 2"-wide band that is long enough to fit around his or her waist and overlap one inch. Invite children to make a skirt to attach to the waistband by taping two sheets of colorful newspaper end to end. Starting at the long side of the newspaper, have students cut 1"-wide strips (or narrow fringes) to within 2" of the other edge. Fold the top down one inch

and staple it between the folds of the waistband. Students can fasten the skirts around their waists with a large paper clip.

Poncho

✔ Newspaper, scissors, heavy tape

Have children cut a vertical and horizontal slit across the center of a double sheet of colorful, glossy newspaper to fit over their heads. Students can place a piece of tape at the end of each slit to prevent tearing. Invite students to wear the ponchos with one corner hanging down in front. (The poncho also makes a great painting smock for a one-time cover-up.)

Cape

✔ Newspaper, scissors, stapler, large paper clips

Invite each student to cut a double sheet of glossy newspaper into a large circle by rounding the corners. Have students cut a slit from one edge to the center of the circle. Have students make newspaper strips to attach to each side of the cape for ties. Staple the ties to the front of the cape. Students can cross the ties in front when wearing the cape and secure together with a paper clip.

Vest

✔ Newspaper, scissors, tape, felt markers, paint

Give each student a double sheet of newspaper folded in half to make a vest. Invite students to cut out a neck hole and two armholes. Reinforce the armholes with tape. Students can use scissors to curve the front for a bolero or cut the front of the vest into points. Invite children to decorate their vests using felt markers or paint.

Dress

✔ Newspaper, tape, scissors, felt markers, paint

Have students tape two double sheets of newspaper together at the short ends. One sheet will hang over the front of their bodies and one over the back, with the taped ends resting on their shoulders. Cut the newspaper in an "A" shape to give the dress a nicer look. Invite students to cut out the neck area to fit over their heads. Students can tape the sides of the dresses, leaving large open areas for armholes. Encourage students to decorate the dresses using felt markers or paint.

Robe

✔ Newspaper, tape, scissors, felt markers, paint, cotton batting, glue

To make a king's robe, students can follow the directions for making a dress, but cut the garment open down the front. Invite students to glue cotton batting around the robe's neck.

Hats

Wet Newspaper Hat

✔ Newspaper, pan of water, liquid starch, bowls (to fit over a child's head), scissors, felt markers, paint

Mix 1/2 cup liquid starch in a pan of water. Completely immerse four double sheets of newspaper (for each hat) in the liquid. Invite students to place one sheet of wet newspaper over an upside-down bowl. Repeat, placing each of the four sheets over the bowl with the corners pointing in different directions. Allow the newspaper-covered bowl to dry in the sun. When completely dry, remove the newspaper hat from the bowl. Students can trim the brim to the desired shape and then paint or decorate each hat.

Floppy Hat

✔ Newspaper, scissors, hole punch, hole reinforcers, yarn or ribbon, glue, felt markers, paint

Invite each student to cut three layers of newspaper into a large oval. Have students glue the edges of the layers together. Punch two holes on opposite sides of the longest sides. Children can strengthen the holes with hole reinforcers. Encourage children to tie lengths of yarn or ribbon through each hole. Students can tie the yarn under their chins when wearing their floppy hats. Encourage students to decorate their hats using felt markers or paint.

Headbands

✔ Newspaper, ribbon, paper flowers, glue, stapler, scissors, construction paper

Invite children to fold a sheet of newspaper to make a 2"-wide band long enough to fit around their heads and overlap slightly. Staple to fit. Encourage children to cut pictures from newspaper or construction paper to glue to the headbands. Children can also add ribbon, paper flowers, and other decorating material.

Folded Newspaper Hat

✔ Newspaper, tape, stapler, pencils

Have each child fold a half sheet of newspaper and place the folded edge at the top. Mark the center of the paper along the folded edge. Have children fold both top corners down to the center line and crease. Tape in place. Fold the bottom edge up twice over the folded triangles. Turn the newspaper over and fold up the bottom edge on the other side so the band is even.

Cone Hat

✔ Newspaper, tape, scissors

Invite each child to roll a large colorful sheet of newspaper into a cone to fit his or her head. Help students tape the ends in place. Have students trim the bottom edge. Encourage students to make a pom-pom tassel for the top of their hats by fringing a small folded piece of newspaper.

Covered Paper Plate

✔ Newspaper, hole punch, paper plates, glue, scissors, pencils

Invite students to cover a paper plate with colorful newspaper. Have students punch two holes on opposite sides of the hat and tie a length of yarn through each hole. Encourage students to add "hair" to their hats by attaching newspaper strips around the edge of the plate. Students can make curls (by wrapping strips around a pencil) or braids.

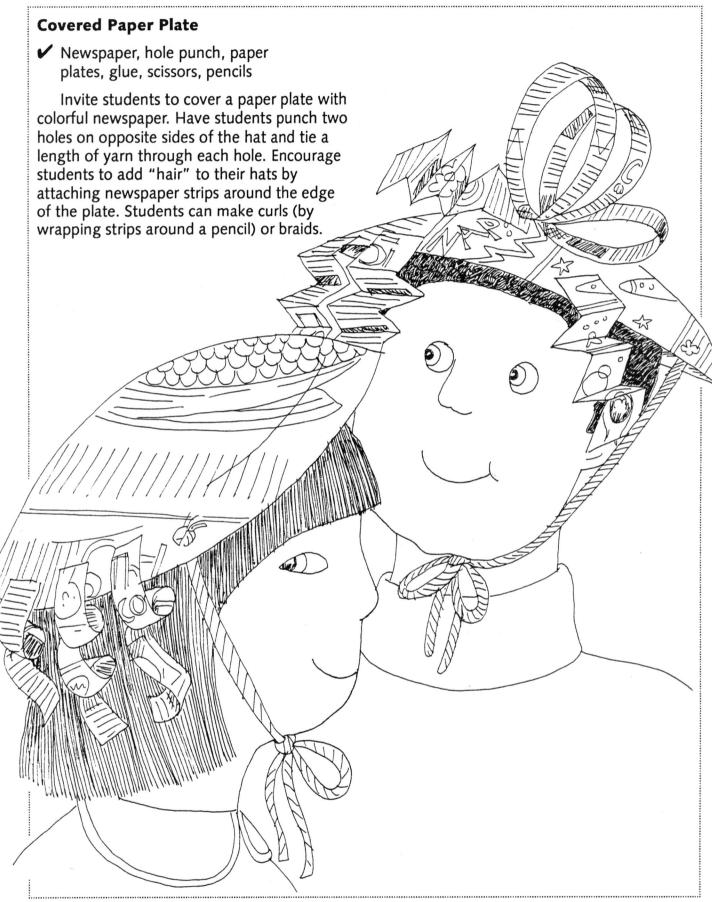

Accessories

Bow Tie or Hair Ribbon

✔ Newspaper, scissors, tape, large paper clips or hairpins

Invite each student to cut a 1 1/2" x 12" strip from colorful newspaper. Have each student fold the strip into thirds and squeeze it together in the middle to create a bow. Students can use tape to hold the bow in place. Invite students to attach the bows to their clothing with a large paper clip or to their hair with a hairpin.

Ribbon Bow

✔ Newspaper, scissors

Invite each student to cut a 1 1/2" x 24" strip from colorful newspaper. Challenge students to carefully tie the paper strip into a bow. Encourage students to try tying bows of varying lengths and widths.

Braided Belt

✔ Newspaper, scissors, tape, stapler, large paper clips

Invite children to cut several 1/2" wide strips from colorful newspaper. Have children tape the strips together to make three strips about 40" long. Stack the strips on top of one another and staple them together at one end. Encourage children to braid the strips and then staple the other ends together. Children can fasten the braided belts around their waists with a large paper clip.

Chain Necklace

✔ Newspaper, tape or glue, scissors, large paper clips

Have children cut several short 1/2" x 2" newspaper strips. Invite children to glue or tape strips into interlocking circles to make a paper chain. Encourage children to fasten the chain necklace loosely around their necks with a large paper clip.

Part II

PAPER BAGS

Since paper bags come in many sizes, shapes, and colors, the possibilities for using this readily available teaching tool are unlimited.

Chapter 7 # Creative Movement with Paper Bags

Paper bags are great movement motivators and children love to use them. Imaginations will soar as children work with these familiar objects in new and surprising ways.

Hop, Skip, and Jump

Dance Partner

✔ Paper bags, music

Give each child a grocery bag. Invite children to hold the bags in front of them as if the bags were dancing partners. Play music and encourage children to move freely.

Three-Leg Walk

✔ Paper bags, yarn

Have each pair of children share one bag. Each puts a foot inside the bag as children stand facing the same direction. Tie the bag loosely around the children's ankles with yarn. Challenge children to walk forward, backward, and sideways. Encourage children to try sliding, moving in circles, and moving in other creative ways in cooperation with their partner.

Me and My Paper Bag

✔ Paper bags

Give each child a paper bag to use as he or she pantomimes the following scenario.

Crush your bag into a ball. Toss it up and catch it. Touch the ball to your heel, your elbow, your neck, your left thigh, and your right ear. Place the crushed bag on the floor. Tiptoe around it. Jump over it three times. Step backward over it. Kneel down and blow it a few inches. Stand up and kick the crushed ball toward the wall. Pick up the ball. Smooth it out flat. Balance it on your head. Turn around four times. Take two giant steps, four tiny steps, two hops, and five jumps. Run in place. Sit down. Take the bag off your head. Use it for a pillow and rest a few minutes.

Bag Balance

✔ Small paper bags, felt markers

Invite each child to decorate a small paper bag using felt markers. Encourage children to balance the bags on their heads while walking, tiptoeing, marching, or taking giant steps. Invite children to create new ways to move while balancing their bags. Encourage children to try balancing their bags on other body parts, such as their shoulders, toes, knees, or elbows.

Home Base

✔ Paper bags

Give each child a bag to use as a home base. Invite children to stand on their bases, slide away from their bases, hop around their bases, jump over their bases, or sit on their bases during story time.

Action Words

✔ Paper bags, felt markers

Write an action word, such as twist, spin, bend, stretch, gallop, or skip, on several bags. Hold up one bag at a time and encourage children to perform the appropriate action.

Animal Movements

✔ Paper bags, scissors, magazines or color books, glue

Cut animal pictures, such as a kangaroo, snail, frog, or rabbit, from magazines or coloring books. Glue one picture to each bag. Hold up one bag at a time and encourage children to imitate each animal's movement.

Over, Under, and Through

Tunnels

✔ Large paper bags, scissors, tape

Give each group of children several large paper bags. Invite children to cut out the bottoms of the bags and smooth the creased edges to form bag tunnels. Encourage children to tape several bags together to make a long tunnel to crawl through. Challenge children to crawl backward through the tunnel. Invite each child to pretend he or she is a caterpillar inside a cocoon (bag tunnel). Invite children to emerge as butterflies.

Movin' On

✔ Paper bags

Invite children to place a bag on the floor in front of them. Challenge children to find a way to move over the bag, around it, on it, and under it.

Bag Props

Toss Bags

✔ Small paper bags, newspaper, stapler

Invite children to help you stuff several small, heavyweight paper bags with torn newspaper strips. Staple the bags shut. Encourage children to toss and catch the stuffed bags.

Basket Bags

✔ Large paper bags, toss bags, felt markers, paint

Fold down the tops of three large paper bags to make baskets. Invite children to practice throwing "toss bags" into the baskets. Paint each basket bag a different color, or write a numeral on each basket bag. Give children directions for throwing. For example, ask children to throw a toss bag into the yellow basket, throw a toss bag into basket #2, and so on.

See-Saw

✔ Paper bags

Invite each pair of children to face one another while each is holding the same bag. One partner bends his or her knees. When that child straightens, the other partner bends his or her knees. Partners can continue alternating the up and down movement. Partners can also sit in a straddle position facing each other and do a push and pull movement.

Bag Ball

✔ Paper bags, felt markers or paint, newspaper, tape, chalk

Insert one bag into another for strength. Decorate the outer bag using felt markers or paint. Stuff the bag with torn newspaper. Fold down the top and tape in place. Invite children to use the bag ball for tossing and catching. Draw different-sized chalk circles and a starting line on the sidewalk. Encourage children to stand behind the start line and slide the bag into one of the circles. Assign point values to each circle. Encourage older children to keep score.

Bag Boots

✔ Paper bags, yarn

Give each child two bags and invite children to wear them over their shoes. Have children tie the bags around their ankles with yarn. Discuss the type of footwear worn for such activities as walking in the snow, climbing a mountain, skiing, ice skating, and horseback riding. Encourage children to pretend they are doing these activities and that their "bag boots" are the appropriate footwear.

Bag Obstacle Courses

Brown Brick Road

✔ Paper bags, tape, scissors

Invite children to help you create a "brown brick road" using paper bags. Use a variety of bag sizes and shapes. For example, arrange 6 to 8 bags with short ends or long ends together in a row. Alternate short and long bags. Separate the road, leaving a space between bags. Combine bag bricks in alternating long and short arrangements. Form obstacles with bags. Place a bag on the table so children can go under the bag. Place a bag on a low box so children can go over the bag. Set up a hopscotch pattern. Include right and left turns, circle patterns, and back tracking. Once the course is completed, encourage children to walk through it. Then invite children to move in other ways through the course as well.

Colors, Letters, Shapes

✔ Paper bags, felt markers, paint, tape, scissors

Use colored bags, bags with numerals written on them, or bags with geometric shapes drawn on them to set up an obstacle course. Give children specific directions for moving through the course. For example, ask children to step on the "A," jump over the blue bag, or stand on one foot inside the triangle.

Footprint Path

✔ Paper bags, paint in shallow container, tub of water, towels

Give each child two paper bags. Invite children to dip their bare feet in paint to make a right footprint on one bag and a left footprint on the other. Have children rinse their feet in a tub of water and dry them. When the prints are dry, set up a footprint path alternating right and left prints. Encourage children to place the appropriate foot on each bag as they move through the course. Create a similar path using handprints. Invite children to move through the path on their hands and knees.

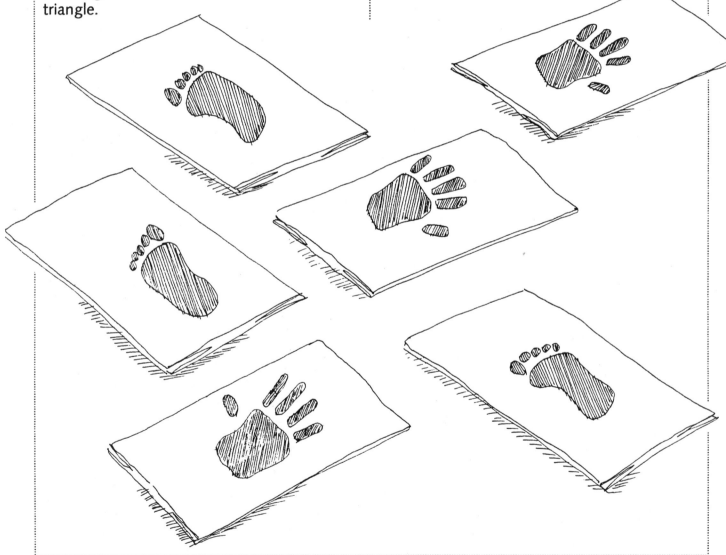

Chapter 8 Language Arts with Paper Bags

Paper bags can become an important teaching tool for your language arts program. Use them to teach idea sequencing, introduce new vocabulary, generate story ideas, and practice word recognition.

Literature

Book Hunt

✔ Paper bag, 3" x 5" cards, pencils

List clues on 3" x 5" cards that describe books in your classroom library. Include such things as the color of a book, the number of words in the title, a description of an illustration, or something about the author. Put all the cards in a paper bag. Invite each student to draw out one card and find the book that is described. Give students opportunities to read the books they have found.

Book Covers

✔ Paper bags, scissors, tape, felt markers

Invite students to use a paper bag to design and make a book cover for their favorite book.

Mystery Book

✔ Paper bag, book

Use a paper bag to introduce a new book. Hide the book in the bag as you describe and introduce it. Then remove it from the bag.

The Three Kittens

✔ Small paper bags, felt markers

Invite children to trace their right hands on one small paper bag and their left hands on another. Have children color their handprints to look like mittens. As you tell or read the story of the three little kittens who lost their mittens, encourage children to pantomime the appropriate actions using their mitten bags.

The Three Little Pigs

✔ Large paper bags, felt markers, scissors, paint, construction paper, glue, yarn

Divide children into groups of four. Have one child place a bag over his or her head while a partner uses a felt marker to carefully mark the place where the child's eyes are located. Have the child remove the bag and cut out eyeholes in the appropriate spots. Invite each child to decorate his or her mask as one of the characters from the story The Three Little Pigs (one of the three pigs or the wolf). Encourage each group to pantomime appropriate actions using their masks as you read or tell the story. Challenge children to make masks for other favorite stories as well (The Three Billy Goats Gruff, Three Blind Mice, and so on).

Wild Things

✔ *Where the Wild Things Are* by Maurice Sendak, paper bags, scissors, felt markers, construction paper, glue

After reading the story *Where the Wild Things Are* by Maurice Sendak, invite each child to make a "wild thing" mask using a paper bag. Reread the book and encourage children to wear their masks and pantomime appropriate actions.

Reading Award Bags

✔ Paper bags, prizes, felt markers, yarn or ribbon

Decorate three bags and number them. Place small prizes, such as pencils, stickers, or small toys, in the bags. Twist and tie the tops with yarn or ribbon. Invite each child to select a prize from one of the bags each time he or she finishes reading a book.

Bag Research

A Bag Is Born

✔ Encyclopedias and other research materials, lined paper, pencils

Encourage children to research the origin of paper, burlap, plastic, cloth, or leather to find out how and where each is manufactured.

Bag Maker

✔ Paper bags, butcher paper, glue, tape, scissors

Invite each student to cut a bag open and carefully examine its construction. Encourage each student to design and make his or her own paper bag as well.

Word List

✔ Paper bags, pencils

Encourage children to think of a list of words or phrases that contain the word *bag* (money bag, tea bag, book bag, handbag, bag of tricks, and so on).

Creative Writing

Story Parts

✔ Paper bags, 3" x 5" cards, pencils, lined paper

Prepare three groups of 3" x 5" cards—main characters, story setting, major problem. Place each set in a separate paper bag. Invite each student or pair of students to select one card from each bag and use the information to create a story.

Story Starters

✔ Paper bags, lined paper, pencils

Brainstorm a list of story titles that involve paper bags and write them on the chalkboard. Invite each student to choose a title and then write a story about a paper bag from the bag's point of view. Suggested titles might include "The Day I Finally Got Out of the Cupboard" or "The Load That Was Too Heavy." Encourage children to use a paper bag as a puppet as they read their stories to the class.

Picture Paragraph

✔ Paper bags, magazines, scissors, glue, pencils

Invite each student to cut a picture from a magazine and glue it to one side of a paper bag. Encourage students to write a paragraph on the other side of the bag that describes the picture.

Tying It All Together

✔ Paper bags, scissors, magazines, lined paper, pencils

Prepare small bags with several magazine pictures in each. Ask each child to choose a bag and carefully look at each picture. Challenge students to write a short story that ties all the pictures together.

Story Add-On

✔ Paper bags, assorted objects

Give each group of children a paper bag containing an interesting or unusual object (fluffy powder puff, stretch watchband, or empty film canister). Invite the first group member to remove the item from the bag and begin telling a story about it. After telling a few sentences, ask the first child to pass the object to the second child. Invite the second child to continue telling the story. Continue passing the object until each student has had a chance to contribute to the story. Remind students that a good story has a beginning, middle, and end.

Chapter 9 Science with Paper Bags

Paper bags are a great resource to stimulate countless science activities. Encourage students to estimate, predict, and make discoveries.

Environment

Litter Bags

✔ Paper bags, felt markers

Invite each child to write or illustrate an anti-litter slogan or message on a bag. Encourage children to pick up litter around the school yard and put it in their bags.

Snack Bags

✔ Small paper bags, trail mix

Fill small paper bags with trail mix or another healthy snack food. Give each child a bag. Invite children to sit outside quietly and look for birds or insects or listen for nature sounds.

Nature Collection

✔ Paper bags, magnifying glasses

Give each child a paper bag to carry as you go on a class nature walk. Encourage children to collect special leaves, rocks, pinecones, or other nature items in their bags. Caution children not to pick flowers or leaves from trees or plants, but to collect only things that have fallen to the ground. When you return to the classroom, invite children to examine their collections more closely under a magnifying glass. Place the treasures on the science table, or use them for art projects.

Bagged Plant

✔ Paper bag, two potted plants

Place two potted plants (the same type and size) side by side. Cover one with a paper bag for three or four days. Uncover the plant after three or four days and invite children to discuss their observations. Continue the experiment by placing the bag back over the plant for several more days. Be sure to water both plants equally.

Exploring Bags

Bags, Bags, Bags

✔ Variety of bags, such as paper bags, plastic bags, waxed bags, cloth bags, insulated bags, laundry bags, ice bags

Ask children what they think the different bags are used for. Explain and discuss the types of bags, what they are made of, and how they are used. Invite children to look for similarities and differences.

Bag Texture

✔ Variety of bags, such as paper bags, plastic bags, waxed bags, cloth bags, insulated bags, laundry bags, ice bags, burlap bags

Encourage children to feel each of the bags in the collection. Discuss the textures (rough, glossy, scratchy, smooth). Challenge students to suggest reasons why all bags are not made of paper. Place the bag collection in a larger bag. Invite children to take turns reaching a hand in the bag and telling the kind of bag (or what it could be used for) that they are touching.

It's in the Bag

✔ Assorted paper bags, water, pencils, balance scales

Give each child a paper bag and a pencil. Have children write the numbers 1 to 4 down the left-hand side of the bag. Invite children to write their answers to the following four questions beside the numerals.

1. Will a paper bag hold air?

2. Does air have weight?

3. Will a paper bag hold water?

4. Will a paper bag absorb water?

After discussing student responses, experiment with the bags to test the predictions.

1. Blow air into a bag and twist the end tightly. Encourage children to feel the bag.

2. Blow air into one bag and twist the top tightly so the air can't escape. Hang the bag on one end of a balance scale. Hang an empty bag (of identical size) on the other end of the scale.

3. Hold a paper bag over a sink or outside

and pour water into it. Repeat using other types of paper bags. Compare the results.

4. Pour a small amount of water onto several different kinds of paper bags.

Sensory Experiences

Touch and Guess

✔ Paper bags, textured materials

Fill a bag with objects made of various materials and textures (fuzzy, plastic, wooden, metal). Invite a child to reach his or her hand in the bag and identify an object by touch alone.

Which Is Heaviest?

✔ Small paper bags, balance scale, yarn, small objects (wooden blocks, crayons, or erasers)

Put an object in each of five bags. Tie each bag closed with yarn. Challenge students to seriate the bags by weight (lightest to heaviest). Invite students to check their ideas by weighing the bags on a balance scale.

Identical Weight

✔ Small paper bags, yarn, balance scale, small objects (wooden blocks, crayons, or erasers)

Put an object in each of five bags. Make two of the bags the same weight. Challenge students to determine which of the two bags weigh the same without using a scale. Invite children to check their prediction by weighing the two bags they think have equal weight.

Sound Bags

✔ Small paper bags, sound items (rice, beans, plastic Legos, crayons, bells), yarn

Prepare ten sound bags. Put identical items in each pair of bags. For example, fill two bags with rice, two with beans, and so on. Tie the tops closed with yarn. Invite children to shake the bags and find the matching pairs.

Musical Bags

✔ Small paper bags, rice, beans, popcorn, yarn, felt markers, paint

Place one bag inside another for strength. Give each child a double bag and invite children to decorate their bags using felt markers or paint. Encourage children to fill their bags with rice, beans, popcorn, or other items. Tie the tops closed with yarn. Invite children to shake their "musical" bags to create rhythm patterns.

Smelly Bags

✔ Small paper bags, cotton balls, perfume, flavor extracts, spice, after-shave lotion, bath powder, yarn

Saturate several cotton balls with perfume, spice, after-shave, and so on. Place each cotton ball in a separate paper bag. Make two bags that smell alike. Tie the top of each bag loosely with a piece of yarn. Invite children to smell the bags and describe or identify the fragrances. Encourage children to find the two bags that smell alike.

Nutrition

Bag Lunch

✔ Paper bags, magazines, scissors, glue, pencils

Invite each student to decide on what foods would make a nutritionally balanced lunch. Encourage children to cut food and beverage pictures from magazines to represent their choices. On a predetermined day, have children bring their pictures in a paper lunch bag. Give each student an opportunity to describe his or her lunch and tell why it is nutritionally balanced.

Predicting

Ice Cube Effects

✔ Assorted paper bags, clothesline, clothespins, ice cubes

Hang three different types of paper bags on a clothesline. Add one ice cube to each bag. Invite children to predict what will happen to each bag as the ice cube melts. Ask students which bag they think will show moisture first, which one will leak first, and if the bottom will fall out of one or more of the bags.

Bag Absorption

✔ Assorted bags, shallow pans, 1-cup measure, timer

Add a cup of water to three shallow pans. Completely immerse a different type of bag in each pan. Set the timer for three minutes. While the bags are soaking, invite students to predict which bag will absorb the most water. After three minutes, remove each bag and allow the excess water to drip into the pan. Pour the water from each pan back into a 1-cup measure. Calculate how much water each bag absorbed and compare it with student predictions.

Bag Evaporation

✔ Assorted bags, tablespoon

Place three different types of bags in direct sun. Pour a tablespoon of water on the center of each bag. Invite students to predict from which bag the water will evaporate first.

Bag Strength

✔ Assorted bags, variety of objects

Select three different types of bags and invite one child to hold the top of each bag open. Encourage other students to take turns adding identical objects to the three bags at the same time. Invite students to predict which bag will hold the heaviest amount of materials and which bag will break first.

Bag Insulation

✔ Assorted paper bags, small plastic bags, twist ties, ice cubes

Place three ice cubes in each of four small plastic bags. Twist and tie the bags closed. Place one bag in each of four different paper bags. Set the timer for five minutes. Invite students to predict which bag will feel the coldest and which will feel the warmest at the end of the time period.

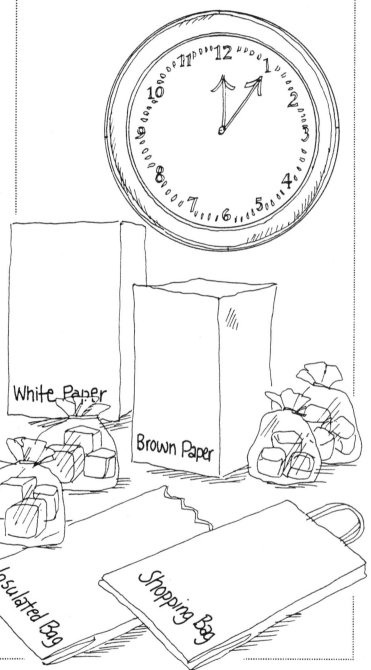

Chapter 10 # Math with Paper Bags

Paper bags can add a new twist to familiar concepts, such as sorting, counting, and classifying. Challenge students to use paper bag manipulatives to practice estimating, calculating, and seriating.

Sorting

Size

✔ Assorted bags

Invite children to sort a collection of bags by size. Graph the results.

Color

✔ Assorted bags

Invite children to sort a collection of bags by color. Encourage children to record the number of bags in each group to determine the largest color group.

Matching

✔ Assorted bags

Challenge children to find matching bags in a collection of assorted bags. For example, invite children to find three bags that are the same size or two bags that have the same shape, but are different colors.

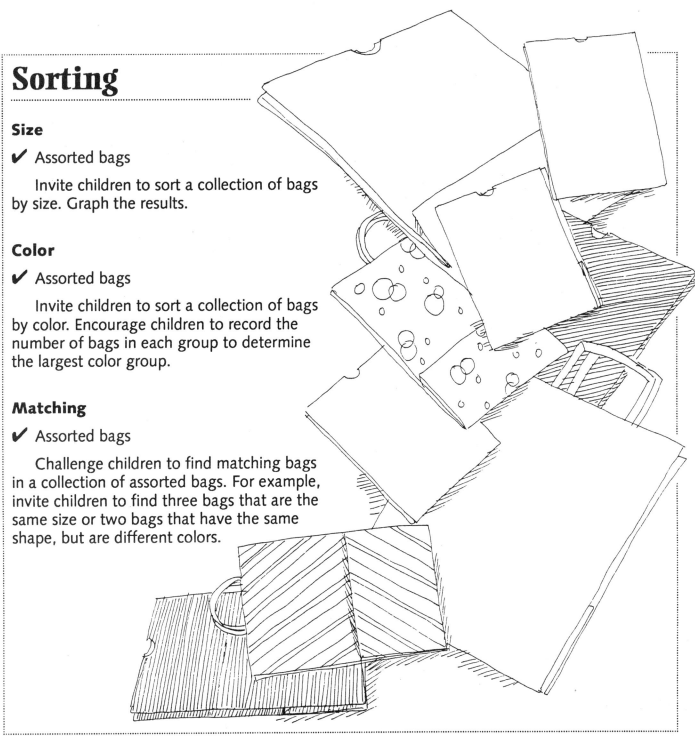

Counting

Count the Bags

✔ Assorted bags

Invite children to count the bags in the collection. Encourage children to count by 2's, 3's, or 5's.

Equal Groups

✔ Assorted bags

Make five groups of bags with each group containing a different number. Invite children to decide how many bags they will need to add or subtract from each group to make the groups equal.

Manipulatives

Number Sequence

✔ Small bags, newspaper, yarn, felt markers

Stuff ten small bags with newspaper. Tie each bag closed with yarn. Using felt markers, number the bags from 1 to 10. Invite children to place the bags in the correct sequence. Once the bags are in counting order, have children close their eyes. Remove one bag. Have children open their eyes and name the missing numbered bag.

Size Sequence

✔ Assorted bags, newspaper, yarn

Using newspaper, stuff several bags of different sizes. Invite children to place the bags in order from largest to smallest.

Fractional Parts

✔ Large paper bags, newspaper, clear plastic cups, water

Give each group of four children four large paper bags, newspaper, and four clear plastic cups. Invite children to stuff the bags with newspaper so that one bag is full, one is 1/2 full, one is 1/3 full, and one is 1/4 full. Invite children to fill the cups with water to represent the same fractional parts.

Money Matters

✔ Paper bags, magazines, scissors, glue, felt markers

Invite children to cut food pictures from magazines and glue each to a stuffed paper bag. Have children write prices on the bags and place the food bags on a classroom shelf. Invite children to "go shopping" and calculate the total price of the items purchased.

Estimating

How Heavy?

✔ Paper bags, counters (bottle caps, beans, or bread tags), notepaper, pencils, scale

Partially fill three paper bags with counters. Roll down the tops of the bags. Invite students to estimate and record how much each bag weighs. Weigh bags and check estimates.

How Many?

✔ Paper bags, counters (bottle caps, beans, or bread tags), notepaper, pencils

Invite each student to place his or her hand in a bag and grab a handful of counters. Have children estimate and record the number of counters they have. Encourage children to count and compare their estimates.

How Full?

✔ Paper bags, large objects, stapler, notepaper, pencils

Place a large object in one paper bag. Place two objects in another paper bag. Place three, four, and five objects in three more bags. Staple the bags closed. Invite children to shake the bags and estimate how many objects are in each one.

Games

Geometric Shapes

✔ Paper bags, geometric shapes

Place several geometric shapes in a bag. You can use commercial geometric blocks or cut geometric shapes from tagboard. Invite children to reach their hands in a bag to find a square, triangle, two shapes that are alike, and so on.

Wrap It Up

✔ Assorted paper bags, classroom objects

Hold up a paper bag and ask children if an object in the classroom would fit inside of it. For example, hold up a lunch bag and ask if a pencil would fit inside. Encourage children to test their responses by actually trying to place the objects in the bag.

Number Patterns

✔ Paper bags, tagboard, felt markers

Make a set of cards numbered from 1 to 10. Place the cards in a bag. Make another set of cards representing the even numbers from 2 to 20 and place them in another bag. Make several other sets of cards, such as multiples of five from 5 to 50, odd numbers from 3 to 30, and multiples of ten from 0 to 100. Place each set in a separate bag. Give each group of children a bag. Ask children to remove the cards from the bag and put them in order. Challenge children to identify each number pattern.

Shape Kids

✔ Paper bags, newspaper, scissors, stapler, felt markers

Invite each child to make a "shape kid" by first cutting a flattened paper bag into a geometric shape. Have children staple around the edges of the two shape pieces, leaving an opening for stuffing. Have children stuff their shapes with paper bag strips or newspaper. Staple the opening closed. Encourage children to draw facial features on one side of each bag. Children can cut paper bag strips to make arms and legs for their shape kids. Invite children to accordion-pleat the strips before stapling them in place.

Chapter 11 # Art with Paper Bags

From leaf rubbings to animal puppets, students will be motivated to create their own unique art and craft projects using paper bags. "Throw-aways" become treasures as junk is transformed into art.

Painting and Coloring

Leaf Rub Prints

✔ Paper bags, leaves, crayons

Invite children to place leaves underneath a lightweight paper bag. Have children rub the side of a crayon over the bag to create leaf rubbings.

Finger Painting

✔ Glossy paper bags, finger paint, scissors

Invite children to cut paper bags open and lay them flat to make smooth finger painting surfaces. Spread finger paint on the opened bag and encourage children to create interesting and unique designs.

Sand Painting

✔ Paper bags, scissors, glue, sand

Have children cut open paper bags and place them flat. Invite children to cut the opened bag into an interesting shape. Encourage children to cover the shapes with a thin layer of glue. Children can cover the glued surface with sand and then shake off any excess. Or, rather than cutting the bag into a shape, students can draw a design with glue and then cover with sand.

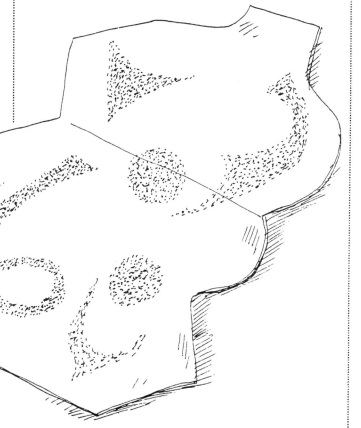

Personalized Art

My Own Bag

✔ Paper bags, felt markers

Invite children to each make a personalized paper bag by writing their names or drawing a self portrait. Children can also add a drawing of their homes or family members. Encourage children to be creative and add other pictures or words that describe who they are.

Gift Wrappings

✔ Paper bags, felt markers or crayons, scissors, paint, ribbon or yarn

Invite each child to create a gift bag for a special friend or family member that they can use the next time they need to wrap a gift. Encourage children to decorate the bag using felt markers, crayons, or paint. Give each child a length of ribbon or yarn to tie the gift bag closed. Or, invite children to cut open a large paper bag and decorate it for wrapping paper.

Smocks

✔ Large paper bags, scissors, felt markers

Cut large neck and armholes in large grocery bags for young children to use as painting smocks. Invite children to draw their initials in a creative way on their smocks.

Picture Frame

✔ Paper bags, scissors, glue

Invite children to cut out the center of a colored paper bag so that the hole is slightly smaller than a picture they would like to frame. Have children glue the edges of the bag to the painting or picture. Hang children's framed artwork on a bulletin board with their names.

Hands

✔ Paper bag, scissors, pencils, felt markers

Invite children to place one hand (fingers spread) on a paper bag so that their middle fingers touch the folded end of the bag. Have children trace around their hands and then cut through both thicknesses of the bag, leaving the fold at the tip of the middle finger. Encourage children to write a list of things they are thankful for inside the hands, or decorate the hands as a Thanksgiving greeting card.

Woven Mats

✔ Paper bags, scissors, tape

Give each child two bags that are the same size, but different colors. Starting at the open end of each bag, have children cut 1"-wide strips through both thicknesses, stopping within 1" of the opposite end of the bags. Invite children to lay one bag horizontally and place the other vertically with the closed end at the top. Children can weave the strips of the vertical bag through the strips of the horizontal bag. Fold the loose ends under and tape in place.

Chalk Texture Pictures

✔ Paper bags, scissors, chalk

Have children cut one side from a paper bag and crush the piece tightly into a ball. Have children smooth out the crushed paper. Invite children to draw pictures or write their names in an interesting way on the wrinkled paper using colored chalk that has been dipped in water.

Mini-Murals

✔ Large paper bags, scissors, pinking shears, paint, felt markers, collage materials, glue

Invite each group of children to cut and open a large paper bag to make a mini-mural. Invite children to work cooperatively to create a scene, design, or collage that represents each person in the group. Use pinking shears to trim the edges.

Collages

Valentine Bags

✔ Paper bags, collage materials (ribbon, doilies, yarn, glitter, construction paper), glue, scissors, stapler

Invite children to glue collage materials to a paper bag to make valentine bags. Children can staple a red strip of construction paper across the top for a handle.

Tile Designs

✔ Paper bags, scissors, construction paper

Cut construction paper into assorted small shapes or tile designs. Invite children to glue the shapes to one side of a flattened paper bag. Encourage children to cover the entire side of the bag by placing the shapes close together.

Collage Covered Bags

✔ Paper bags, collage materials (ribbon, felt, yarn, buttons, glitter), glue, scissors

Invite each child to decorate a paper bag with collage materials. Have an art show and display the finished work.

Junk Art

Litter Collages

✔ Paper bags, glue, stapler

Give each student a paper bag to pick up litter in the school yard or on a walk around the block. After returning to the classroom, invite children to arrange and glue or staple the litter to one side of the paper bag. Display the litter collages on a bulletin board with an anti-litter message.

Recycling Ideas

✔ Paper bags, recyclable odds and ends, glue, scissors, felt markers

Invite each student to bring a paper bag from home that is full of small "throw-away" items (plastic lids, margarine tubs, small plastic bottles, egg cartons, and bottle caps). Discuss possibilities for recycling the items into art or craft projects. Encourage students to be creative as they use the materials to create a work of art.

Throw-Away Fun

✔ Large paper bags

Set five large paper bags in the front of the classroom. Invite children to help you decide what "throw-away" items they could collect in each bag. For example, they could collect old greeting cards in one bag, used ribbon in another, and juice boxes in a third. After the bags are full, write a day of the week on each bag. On that day, distribute the contents of the bag to students to use for the day's creative art project.

Stuffed Bag Projects

Jack-o'-Lantern

✔ Paper bags, newspaper, orange and green paint, felt markers, green yarn

Invite each child to paint the bottom 3/4 of a bag orange and the top 1/4 green. Allow the bags to dry thoroughly. Have children draw pumpkin facial features on one side of the orange bags using felt markers. Invite children to stuff the bags with newspaper up to the top of the orange section. Have children tie the bags closed with green yarn where the orange and green paint meet.

Doll Puppet

✔ Small paper bags, newspaper, yarn, felt markers, scissors, glue

Invite each child to stuff the end of a small bag and tie it off tightly with yarn to form a doll head. Encourage children to add facial features and yarn hair. Children can draw clothes on the remaining bag using felt markers. Cut two small armholes on each side of the bag. Have children put their hands up into the bag inserting their index fingers into the doll's head. Have children put their thumbs and little fingers into the armholes to move the puppet.

Pillow

✔ Paper bags, newspaper, stapler, hole punch, yarn

Invite each child to stuff a colored paper bag with newspaper. Staple the end closed. Punch holes around the four sides of the bag. Invite children to lace yarn through the holes.

Leggy Creatures

✔ Paper bags, newspaper, scissors, stapler, paint, felt markers, glue

Invite children to create a ladybug, spider, or other leggy creature by stuffing and painting a paper bag body. Have children add accordion-pleated legs made from paper bag strips. Encourage children to draw features using felt markers, or cut features from colored paper bags and glue in place.

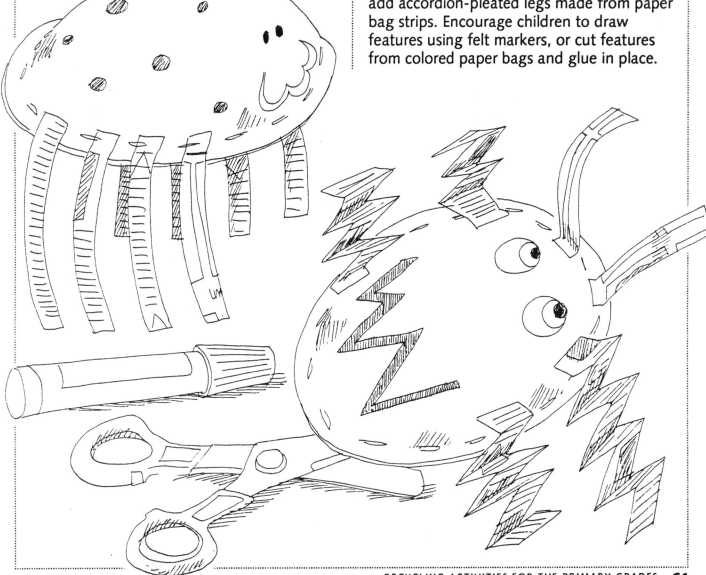

Animals

Clothespin Creatures

✔ Paper bags, glue, clothespins, felt markers, scissors

Invite children to cut an animal face and body from a double thickness of paper bag. Have children glue the edges together and decorate as desired. Clip two clothespins on the bottom for legs and the animal will stand.

Turkey

✔ Paper bags, scissors, stapler, newspaper, glue, clothespins, felt markers

Have children cut two identical circles from a brown paper bag. Staple the two circles together around the edge leaving a small opening. Invite children to stuff the circle and staple the opening closed. Children can cut feathers from the rest of the bag and color them with felt markers. Staple the feathers across the top edge of the circle on the back side. Children can cut a turkey head from the paper bag, add details, and glue it to the center front of the stuffed circle. Invite children to add two pinch-type clothespins for legs.

Animal Faces

✔ Paper bags, scissors, stapler, newspaper, glue, felt markers, construction paper

Have children cut two identical circles from a brown paper bag. Staple the two circles together around the edge leaving a small opening. Invite children to stuff the circle and staple the opening closed. Invite children to add details using felt markers to make a lion, bear, elephant, or other animal face. Children can glue the animal faces to a large sheet of construction paper and draw grass, trees, river, or other surroundings.

Rabbit

✔ Paper bags, scissors, newspaper, yarn, cotton balls, felt markers, glue

Invite each child to loosely stuff a brown or white paper bag. Have children tie a piece of yarn around the middle of the bag tightly enough to separate the body into two parts. Tie the top of the bag closed. Encourage children to add a cotton tail, ears cut from a paper bag, and facial features.

Cat

✔ Paper bags, newspaper, scissors, yarn, felt markers, glue

Invite each child to loosely stuff a brown or white paper bag. Have children tie a piece of yarn around the middle of the bag tightly enough to separate the body into two parts. Tie the top of the bag closed. Encourage children to add a yarn tail, ears cut from a paper bag, and facial features.

Chapter 12 # Dramatic Play with Paper Bags

Since paper bags come in a variety of colors, shapes, and sizes, they lend themselves well to the creation of simple costumes. These innovative props will add interest and color to dramatic play, creative drama, nursery rhymes, and poems.

Costumes

Space Suit

✔ Assorted paper bags, yarn, scissors, paint, tape, felt markers, construction paper, glue

Encourage students to use an assortment of paper bags to create space suits. Children can slip two matching bags over their shoes and tie the bags with yarn around their ankles. To make sleeves, suggest that children cut the bottoms out of two matching bags and fit the bags over their arms. Help children tie the bags with yarn at their wrists. Invite children to make helmets by cutting a large window out of a large paper bag and placing it over their heads. Encourage students to paint and decorate their suits. Challenge children to make a suit of armor or use bags to dress up as a robot.

Hula Skirt

✔ Large paper bags, scissors, large paper clips

Using bags large enough to fit around their waists, invite children to cut down one seam and cut out the bag's bottom. Have children fold down one long edge about 1" to make a waistband. Starting at the other long edge, children can cut slits up the skirt to within 2" of the waistband. Invite children to wear their skirts by securing them around their waists with a large paper clip.

Shirt or Vest

✔ Large paper bags, scissors, felt markers, magazines, paint, glue

Have children cut down one seam of a large grocery bag and then cut out the bottom. Help children cut armholes on each side of the flattened bag in the appropriate spots. Encourage children to decorate their shirts using felt markers, paint, or pictures cut from magazines. Children can fringe the edges or round the bottom front corners. For a leather look, invite children to spray the shirt with water, crush it into a ball, and smooth it out on a flat surface.

Hats and Masks

Beanie

✔ Paper bags, scissors, yarn or ribbon, felt markers

Help children find bags that fit their heads. Have children cut off the bottom ends of the bags. Invite children to twist the top and tie it with a piece of ribbon or yarn. Children can fringe or scallop the ends of the twist. Have each child cut off the open end of the bag leaving just enough to turn up for a cuff. Encourage children to decorate their beanies.

Mask

✔ Large paper bags, felt markers, scissors, paint, construction paper, glue, yarn, cotton balls

Have one child place a bag over his or her head while a partner uses a felt marker to carefully mark the place where the child's eyes are located. Have the child remove the bag and cut out eyeholes in the appropriate spots. Invite children to decorate their masks as they desire. Children can cut facial features from construction paper. Encourage children to make hair using yarn or fringed paper. Children can cut a collar to make a clown mask or add cotton balls to make a lamb. Encourage creativity. You may need to trim the bag so it will rest easily on top of the child's shoulders.

Circus Cone Hat

✔ Large paper bags, tape, crepe paper, felt markers

Give each child a large paper bag to cut open and roll into a cone shape. Have children tape the cone in place. Children can turn up the bottom to form a cuff. Encourage children to add crepe paper pom-poms to the top and decorate as desired.

Crown

✔ Paper bags, scissors, stapler, felt markers, glitter, glue

Have children cut open a paper bag and turn up the end to form a cuff. Help each child fit the opened bag around his or her head, trim to desired length, and staple the edges. Invite children to trim the edges of their crowns to make scallops, fringes, or points. Encourage children to decorate their crowns using felt markers and glitter.

Headbands

✔ Paper bags, scissors, stapler, tape, glue, magazines, construction paper

Invite children to cut wide strips from paper bags long enough to fit around their heads and overlap slightly. Encourage students to fold strips two or three times for added strength. Help children fit and staple the headbands to the appropriate size. Invite children to cut pictures from magazines or trace patterns on construction paper to glue to their headbands.

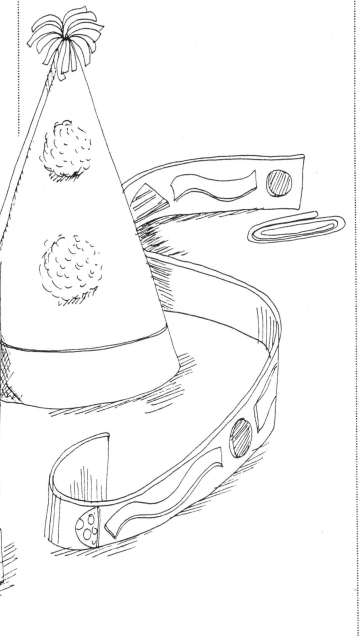

Accessories

Boots

✔ Paper bags, scissors, felt markers, yarn

Invite children to fit a bag over each shoe and loosely tie yarn around their ankles to secure the bags. Children can use felt markers to draw lacing holes and shoelaces. Encourage children to pantomime walking, skipping, hopping, prancing, and hiking.

Bow Ties

✔ Paper bags, scissors, tape, paper clips, hairpins

Invite children to cut strips from colored paper bags and fold them to make bows. Children can attach the bows to their clothing with paper clips or use hairpins to wear the bows in their hair.

Belts

✔ Paper bags, scissors, tape, paper clips

Invite children to cut strips from colored paper bags and tape them together to fit around their waists. Children can attach three long strips together and braid a belt. Or, students can twist two different colored strips together. Invite children to fasten the belts around their waists with paper clips.

Jewelry

✔ Paper bags, scissors, tape, stapler

Invite children to cut short strips from colored paper bags. Children can staple or tape the strips into interlocking circles to make a chain necklace or bracelet.

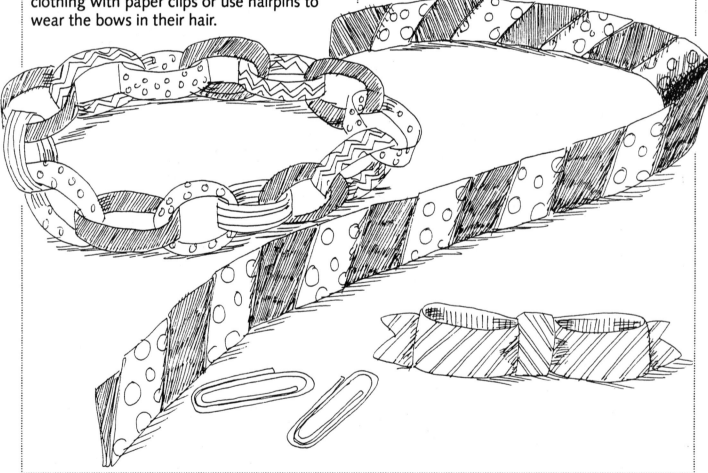

Part III

BOXES AND CARTONS

A simple box or carton can be easily transformed into a castle, train, obstacle course, or an entire city. A never-ending supply of boxes and cartons means creative, social, and educational experiences for young children.

Chapter 13 # Creative Movement with Boxes and Cartons

Small and large muscle activity is fostered through play with boxes and cartons. Movement and exercise are more enjoyable when a tangible object, such as a box, can be held, manipulated, decorated, or transformed into an object.

Box Props

Box and Body

✔ Small boxes

Give children a box to hold in each hand. Give directions for movement. For example, invite children to move their boxes over their heads, to their shoulders, to their hips, and to the floor. Give directions for moving one side of the body or one hand at a time.

In, Out, and All Around

✔ Large boxes

Give each child a box large enough to sit in. Give directions for movement. For example, invite children to step into the box, step over the box, or sit in the box. Encourage children to turn the box upside down and create other movement ideas.

Race Track

✔ Oatmeal or salt containers, yarn

Make a track by placing two parallel pieces of yarn across the classroom floor or play area. Invite children to roll round containers down the track. Children can roll the containers with both hands, right or left hand only, or alternating hands. Challenge children to push the containers with their foreheads. Make target shapes on the track and encourage children to roll the containers to the targets. Invite children to suggest other methods of rolling the containers down the yarn track, too.

Me and My Box

✔ Shoe boxes, gift paper, tape, scissors

Invite children to stand in a circle. Place a shoe box in front of each child. Encourage children to pantomime appropriate actions as you describe the following scenario.

You are walking along and your foot hits a box. Pick it up, look it over, and smell it. Place your box on the floor. Roll it, push it, pull it. Slide the box between your feet, across your toes, and against your heels. Move the box in front of your right foot. Your box is very heavy. Pick it up and slowly, slowly lift it. Hold it on your stomach. Watch the water leak out the bottom of the box. Your box is now very light. Quickly raise it over your head. Rest your box on your knees. Spin around with your box. Place the box on your head, walk forward on tiptoe, and then take a giant step backward. Remove the box from your head. Place it on the floor behind you. Turn around and sit down by your box. Wrap your box in gift paper. Tie it with a ribbon. Pass it to the person on your left. Untie the ribbon on your new box, unwrap it, and look inside. If it is food, eat it. If your new box has clothing, wear it. If your new box has a toy inside, play with it.

Games

Jack-in-the-Box

✔ Large boxes

Give each child a box big enough to sit in. Say the following chant as children squat in and jump out of their boxes. Substitute a child's name for "Jack."

Jack-in-the-Box, quiet as a mouse,

Deep inside your little box house.

Jack-in-the-Box, resting so still,

Will you come out? Yes, I will (pop up).

Bowling

✔ Milk cartons, newspaper, stapler, ball, chalk, construction paper, glue

Stuff several milk cartons with newspaper and staple the tops. Set the cartons in a row. Draw a circle around each carton to mark the place it should be returned to for each setup. Draw a line, several feet from the row of cartons, for students to stand behind. Encourage students to take turns rolling a ball towards the cartons to knock them over. Glue letters, numerals, or shapes to the sides of the cartons. Challenge students to aim at a specific carton. Assign point values to each carton. Encourage older students to keep score.

Building Blocks

✔ Milk cartons, scissors, adhesive-backed paper

Open the tops of the milk cartons. Push the open end of one carton into another carton. Cover the cartons with colorful, adhesive-backed paper. Encourage children to use the colored milk cartons as building blocks.

Ball Roll

✔ Large box, felt markers, ball, scissors

Turn a large box upside down. Cut out geometric shapes along the bottom. Encourage children to roll a ball through the openings. Outline the shapes with felt marker.

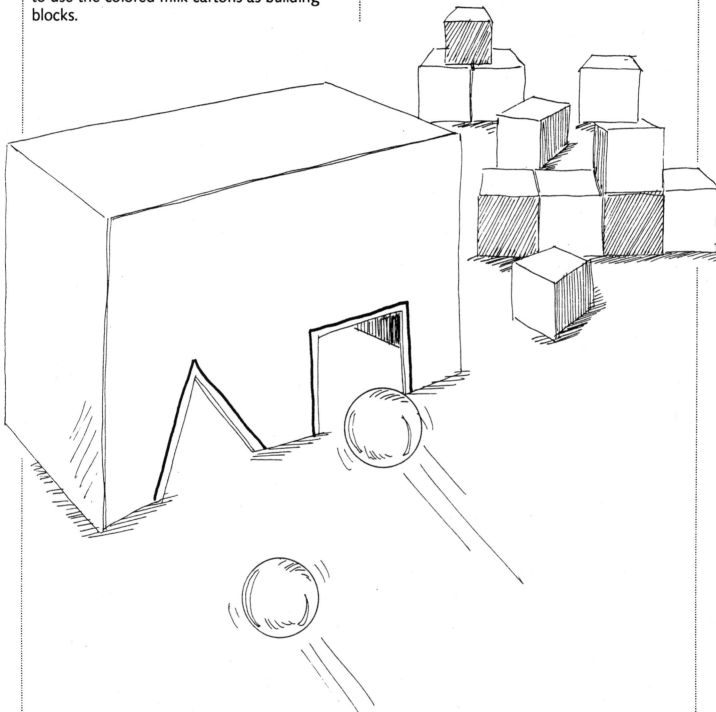

Beanbag Toss

✔ Large box, scissors, beanbags

Turn a large box upside down. Cut out geometric shapes in the top of the box. Invite children to toss beanbags into the openings from various distances.

Beat the Drum

✔ Round cartons (oatmeal, salt, or ice cream), paint, adhesive-backed paper

Invite children to paint or cover a round carton with adhesive-backed paper to use as a drum. Invite a child to beat his or her drum while other children move freely. Challenge children to "freeze" when the drummer stops beating.

Follow the Leader

✔ Boxes

Give each child a box and discuss different movements that can be done with a box. Invite one child to be the leader and lead the group in creative movements. Give each child a chance to be the leader.

Moving Along

Tunnel

✔ Large appliance boxes, duct tape

Cut the ends from two or three large appliance boxes. Tape the boxes together using heavy duct tape to make a long tunnel. Invite children to crawl forward and backward through the tunnel.

Train

✔ Boxes, paint, cord, glue, stapler, scissors

Invite children to paint as many boxes as needed to make a train the desired length. When dry, place in a line. To make an engine, invert a smaller box and attach it to the front of a larger box. Use a smaller box for the caboose. When the boxes are dry, place them in a line and couple the train cars together with cord.

Spaceship

✔ Large appliance box, smaller boxes, tape, scissors, blue plastic wrap

Turn a large appliance box upside down. Tape a smaller square box on top. Make a cone from a lightweight cardboard box and tape it to the top of the second box. Cut a hinged door on the front of the box and a small window in the back. Tape three layers of heavy, blue plastic wrap over the window. Cut two triangles from a cardboard box and tape one to each side of the largest box. Invite students to help paint and decorate the spaceship.

Box Obstacle Courses

Red Arrow Course

✔ Box tunnel, boxes, red paint, scissors

Combine the box tunnel with additional boxes to create an obstacle course. Invite children to explore the course by moving through it going forward and backward. Cut arrows from cardboard and paint them red to indicate directions for moving around, over, into, and through.

Shoe Box Trail

✔ Shoe boxes and lids, construction paper, felt markers, tape, scissors

Tape shoe boxes and shoe box lids around the room to create a trail for students to follow. Invite children to make hand and footprints from construction paper. Place the prints inside the boxes and lids to indicate which foot or hand students are to use as they move through the trail.

Shape Frames

✔ Large appliance boxes, scissors, paint

Cut large, geometric shapes from appliance boxes. Cut the center out of each shape so a 5" frame remains. Invite children to help paint the frames and shapes. Place the shapes around the classroom or play area and lean the frames up against walls and tables or chairs. Give directions for children to move on and through the shapes. For example, invite children to crawl through the green triangle or to tiptoe across the yellow square.

Chapter 14 Language Arts with Boxes and Cartons

Boxes and cartons can stimulate creative thinking and cognitive growth. Boxes and cartons offer opportunities for developing language skills, introducing new vocabulary, and reading.

Creative Writing

Story Starters

✔ Assorted boxes, lined paper, pencils

Display a collection of boxes and invite children to brainstorm story-starter ideas about boxes. For example, students could write a story entitled "The Day I Was Stuck in a Box" or "The Box That Started Talking." Write students' ideas on the chalkboard. Encourage each student to choose an idea and develop it into a creative story.

Poetry

✔ Assorted boxes, lined paper, pencils

Invite students to select a favorite box and write a poem about it. Encourage children to share their poems with the class.

Ad Campaign

✔ Assorted boxes, lined paper, pencils

Invite children to write a classified ad describing a box for sale. Or, students might like to design a logo, slogan, or box ad.

It's in the Mail

✔ Assorted boxes, lined paper, pencils

Encourage students to write a letter to a friend describing a mystery box they received in the mail. Encourage creativity and inventive ideas.

Read and Spell

Read and Find Out

✔ Boxes from familiar products (cereal, toothpaste, cookies)

Place boxes in a large pile. Invite each child to choose a box and tell what came in the box and how they know this. Help children identify words on the box.

Salt Tray

✔ Shallow box, plastic wrap, salt

Line a shallow box with clear plastic wrap. Cover the bottom of the box with a layer of salt. Invite children to draw letters, shapes, and numerals in the salt with their fingers.

Find the Word

✔ Boxes from familiar products (cereal, toothpaste, cookies), notepaper, pencils

Write a word that can be found on one of the boxes in your collection on a piece of notepaper. Make enough word papers for each student and place them in a colorful box. Pile the boxes on a table. Invite each child to choose a slip of paper, read the word, and find a box that has the matching word on it.

Spelling List

✔ Boxes from familiar products (cereal, toothpaste, cookies)

Invite each child to choose a word from a box to help compile a class spelling list.

Name and Number

✔ Boxes from familiar products (cereal, toothpaste, cookies), scissors, construction paper, glue

Invite children to cut out letters from boxes to spell their names. Have children glue the letters in order on a sheet of construction paper. Encourage children to cut out and glue the digits in their telephone numbers, too.

Alphabet Hunt

✔ Boxes from familiar products (cereal, toothpaste, cookies), scissors

Assign each child a letter of the alphabet. Invite children to cut that letter from a box. Help children place all of the letters on a long table, one at a time, in alphabetical order.

Box Letters

✔ Assorted small boxes

Invite children to work in small groups to spell words using boxes to outline the letters. Invite other groups to read the messages spelled with boxes.

Oral Expression

Meet My Box

✔ Assorted boxes

Invite each child to select a box and tell the class five things about the box they chose.

Adjective Alert

✔ Assorted boxes

Invite each child to choose a box and use three adjectives in a sentence to describe the box.

Same or Different?

✔ Assorted boxes

Invite each child to choose a box and then work with a partner. Invite one child to describe how the two boxes are alike, while the other child describes how they are different.

Guess My Box

✔ Assorted boxes

Pile the collection of boxes on a table. Invite children to take turns describing a box from the pile without touching it. For example, a student might begin "I'm thinking of a box that…" Encourage students to point out the box that is being described.

Chapter 15 Science with Boxes and Cartons

Young children will make interesting discoveries and develop new science concepts when provided with a variety of interesting and unusual boxes and cartons to investigate.

Exploring Boxes

Box Attributes

✔ Assorted small boxes

Display a variety of small boxes on a table. Invite children to investigate the collection. Encourage children to sort boxes by what they are made of, their texture, their size, or their color. Encourage children to compare box lids. Place removable box lids in a shoe box and put the matching boxes in a pile nearby. Challenge children to match the boxes with the correct lids.

Sound Boxes

✔ Small boxes, colorful adhesive-backed paper, sound objects (beans, marbles, bells, popcorn)

Invite small groups of children to cover five boxes with the same colorful adhesive-backed paper so that the boxes all look alike. Invite children to add sound objects to each box. For example, children might fill one box with beans, one with popcorn kernels, and one with marbles. Encourage children to fill two boxes with the same objects. Invite children to take turns shaking the boxes and identifying the contents. Challenge children to find the two boxes that sound alike. Invite children to use the sound boxes as musical instruments by shaking them to create rhythms.

Music Box

✔ Boxes, rubber bands

Give each child a box with one open side. Invite children to stretch rubber bands around the box. Have the children pluck the rubber bands. Encourage children to notice that different sounds can be produced with different box depths and sizes of rubber bands.

Weight Boxes

✔ Small boxes, colorful adhesive-backed paper, objects of various weights

Invite small groups of children to cover five boxes with the same colorful adhesive-backed paper so that the boxes all look alike. Invite children to add a different object to each box so that each box has a different weight. Challenge students to seriate the boxes from lightest to heaviest.

Listening Boxes

✔ Assorted boxes, marbles

Invite children to drop marbles into the boxes (wooden, metal, cardboard) and to observe the sound they make. After everyone has had a turn, place boxes out of sight and drop a marble into one of them. Challenge children to identify which box you dropped the marble into. Repeat with the other boxes.

Shape Boxes

✔ Round ice-cream carton, scissors, plastic lids, adhesive-backed paper

Cover an ice-cream container with adhesive-backed paper. Cut geometric shapes in the lid. Cut matching geometric shapes from plastic lids. Invite children to drop the plastic shapes into the matching cutout shapes in the carton.

Box Experiments

Estimating

✔ Large box, notepaper, pencils

Place a large box in a place where all children can see it. Invite students to predict the number of children that could sit in the box at the same time and write their estimates on notepaper. Have children, one at a time, climb into the box and sit down. Hold the box so it doesn't tip over. Count the children in the box and compare the actual number to the estimates.

Predicting

✔ Assorted boxes and cartons, water

Set out an assortment of boxes and cartons. Encourage children to predict which ones will hold water. Take the boxes and cartons outside and invite children to help fill them with water to test their predictions. Discuss absorption.

Floating Boxes

✔ Assorted boxes and cartons, tub of water

Set out an assortment of boxes, cartons, and a tub of water. Encourage children to predict which boxes and cartons will float. Invite children to place the boxes and cartons in the tub of water to test their predictions.

Surprise Boxes

✔ Boxes with lids, science materials (magnets, prisms, magnifying glasses), recycled gift wrap and ribbon, tape

Fill each box with a magnet, prism, magnifying glass, or other science materials. Wrap the boxes in recycled gift paper and tie with a used ribbon. Each day, introduce a science activity by inviting a child to unwrap a different box.

Color Creation Cartons

✔ Yogurt or cottage cheese cartons, water, food coloring

Invite each pair of children to fill a plastic carton 1/4 full of water. Have children add a few drops of two different food colorings to discover new colors they can make.

Creative Thinking

✔ Egg carton lids, small rubber balls

Place a small rubber ball in the center of an egg carton lid. Challenge students to think of ways they can make the ball move without touching it. Children may suggest tipping or shaking the lid, pounding on the table, or blowing on the ball.

Environment

Guest Home

✔ Boxes, newspaper, plastic screen, tape

Line a deep box with several layers of newspaper. Place a frog, lizard, or other small animal in the box for a short while. Cover the top with a plastic screen and tape securely in place. Be sure to provide water and appropriate food for your classroom "guest." Release the animal to its natural habitat.

Bird Feeder

✔ Oatmeal or salt box, wooden skewers, bird seed, scissors, hole punch, string

Cut an oatmeal or salt box down so that it is about 3" tall. Push a wooden skewer through the box just below the top edge. Let the stick extend beyond the box to provide a perch on each side. Punch a hole on each side of the container and tie a piece of string through each one. Fill the shallow container with wild bird seed. Tie the strings around a tree branch. Invite children to observe their feasting feathered friends.

Insect Observation

✔ Milk cartons, scissors, heavy plastic wrap, tape, rocks, sticks, green leaves, insects, stapler

Cut windows from the four sides of a milk carton, leaving just a frame. Cover the windows with heavy plastic wrap and tape in place. Put small rocks, a stick, and some green leaves in the bottom of the carton. Punch small air holes in the box. Add insects, such as ladybugs, beetles, and caterpillars. Staple the top closed. Invite students to observe the insects for a day or two and then release them to their natural environment.

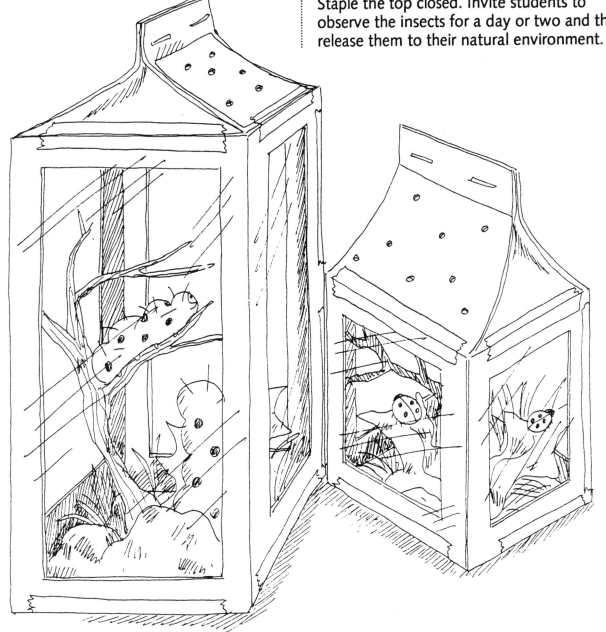

Creepers and Crawlers

✔ Box, plastic wrap or aluminum foil, scissors, soil, dead leaves, rocks, cheesecloth, tape

Line the bottom of a box with heavy plastic wrap or aluminum foil. Cut the box down so it is about 6" high. Cover the bottom of the box with about 2" of moist soil. Add a few dead leaves and a few rocks. Add earthworms, snails, slugs, pill bugs, or other small creatures. Cover the top of the box with cheesecloth and tape in place. Invite children to observe the tiny creatures for a day or two and then release them to their natural habitat.

Plant Boxes

✔ Boxes (with plastic coating inside), heavy plastic wrap or aluminum foil, sand, potting soil, seeds

Invite children to help line a flat box with heavy plastic wrap or aluminum foil or use a fruit box with a plastic-coated bottom. Cover the bottom of each box with 1" of sand. Add a 2" layer of potting soil. Have children plant seeds as directed on the package. Set the box in a sunny place and keep the soil moist. When the plants are about 4" high, transplant them to pots or to an outdoor garden.

Sensory Experiences

Sandbox

✔ Box (with plastic coating inside), small boxes, heavy plastic wrap or aluminum foil, sand, seashells, rocks, yogurt or cottage cheese cartons

Make a large sandbox by filling a fruit box, that has a plastic coating inside, with sand. If the box you are using does not have a plastic coating, line the box with plastic wrap or aluminum foil. Add small boxes of various shapes to the sandbox for pouring and measuring sand. Discuss the terms *full*, *empty*, *half-full*, *light*, and *heavy*. Invite children to pour and measure sand. Invite children to feel under the sand to find treasures. For example, ask children to find one rock, two shells, or one rock and one shell. Moisten the sand and encourage children to build sand castles using yogurt or cottage cheese cartons as molds.

Cornmeal Box

✔ Boxes (with plastic coating inside), heavy plastic wrap or aluminum foil, cornmeal (yellow and white)

Fill one fruit box, that has a plastic coating inside, with white cornmeal and one with yellow cornmeal. If the boxes you are using do not have a plastic coating, line them with plastic wrap or aluminum foil. Add small boxes of various shapes to the boxes for pouring and measuring.

Bean Box

✔ Shallow box, beans, egg cartons, plastic spoons, small boxes

Fill the shallow box with an assortment of beans. Provide egg carton cup sections, plastic spoons, and small boxes. Invite children to pour, fill, and measure.

Playdough

✔ Shallow box, heavy plastic wrap or aluminum foil, flour, salt, water, food coloring or flavoring, and spices

Line a shallow box with heavy plastic wrap or aluminum foil. Add two parts flour and one part salt to the box. Invite children to slowly add water and mix until the mixture becomes a workable dough. Add food coloring or flavoring. Spices could be added to the flour and salt before they are mixed with water.

Magical Mixture

✔ Shallow box, heavy plastic wrap or aluminum foil, cornstarch, water

Line a shallow box with heavy plastic wrap or aluminum foil. Pour in a box of cornstarch. Invite children to slowly add water and mix with their hands. Add just enough water so mixtures oozes and runs through your fingers when picked up and squeezed. A fascinating tactile experience!

Chapter 16 Math with Boxes and Cartons

A collection of boxes and cartons in different sizes and shapes can make great math tools. Boxes and cartons can also be used to make games, introduce counting and grouping, and reinforce beginning math activities.

Graphing

Box Graphs

✔ Assorted boxes, tagboard, felt markers

Encourage children to collect an assortment of boxes. Discuss different ways the collection could be graphed (color, shape, size, material). Invite children to work in pairs or in small groups to create graphs that represent their box collections.

Giant Graph

✔ Assorted boxes, chalk

Use chalk to make a giant graph on the playground blacktop to represent the students' box collection.

Measuring

Measuring Tools

✔ Assorted boxes

Invite each child to choose a box to use as a measuring tool. Encourage students to measure an object in the room using their boxes.

Size Match

✔ Assorted boxes, rulers, paint

Invite children to measure the length of the assortment of boxes. Challenge children to find one 12" box, two 6" boxes, three 4" boxes, and four 3" boxes. Invite children to paint each size a different color. When the boxes are dry, encourage children to use the boxes to answer such questions as "How many red (4") boxes do we need to equal the length of the blue (12") box?"

Calculations

Shoe Box Math

✔ Shoe boxes, clothespins, paint

Give each child a shoe box (with the lid removed) and a collection of colored clothespins. Use colored plastic clothespins or paint wooden clothespins. Invite children to clip the clothespins around the edge of the box in a color pattern. Or, give students a specific pattern to make. Invite students to use the clothespins as manipulatives to solve math problems. For example, ask children to clip on two pins and then add three more. Ask children how many pins are clipped altogether.

Egg Carton Math

✔ Egg cartons, scissors

Invite children to watch as you cut apart egg cup cartons. Demonstrate how a dozen (12) cups can be divided into two groups of six (show both ways), three groups of four, and four groups of three.

Weighing

Balance Scale

✔ Boxes, balance scale, wire hangers, hole punch, string, tape

Make a balance scale using a wire hanger and two identical boxes with the lids removed. Hang the coat hanger in a secure place. Punch holes, at equal distances, on all four sides near the top of the boxes. Cut eight equal lengths of string. Tie a piece of string through each hole and knot it. Tie the four strings together. Tie one box at each end of the coat hanger so the scale balances. Tape the string to the hanger.

Which Weighs More?

✔ Assorted small boxes, balance scale, felt markers

Invite each child to select two boxes from an assorted collection. Ask children to predict which box weighs the most and make an "x" on it. Encourage children to weigh their boxes on the balance scale (from the previous activity) to test their predictions. Invite children to weigh other classroom objects as well.

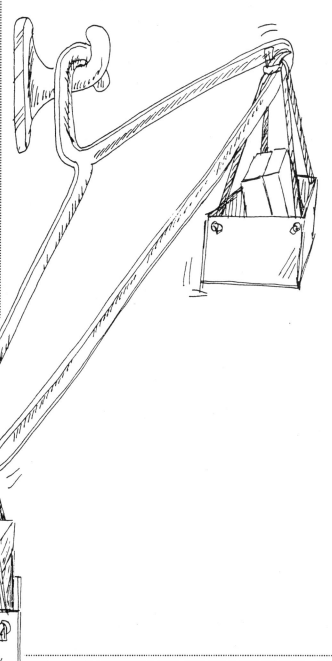

Games

Match the Box

✔ Assorted boxes, felt markers, cardboard, colorful butcher paper, tape

Trace an outline of each box on a piece of cardboard cut from a large box. After tracing the boxes, place them in a larger box covered with colorful paper. Invite children to match the boxes with their outlines.

Find the Box

✔ Assorted small boxes

Pile a collection of small boxes on the floor between two rows of children. Have partners sit facing each other. Have one partner take a box from the pile and ask his or her partner to find a smaller box, a larger box, a shorter box, and so on.

Largest to Smallest

✔ Assorted boxes

Invite children to sit in a circle and give each child a box. Ask the child who has the largest box to place it in the center of the circle. Ask the child who has the second largest box to also place it in the circle. Continue until each child has placed his or her box in the circle and the boxes are seriated by size. You might want to start this activity with smaller groups.

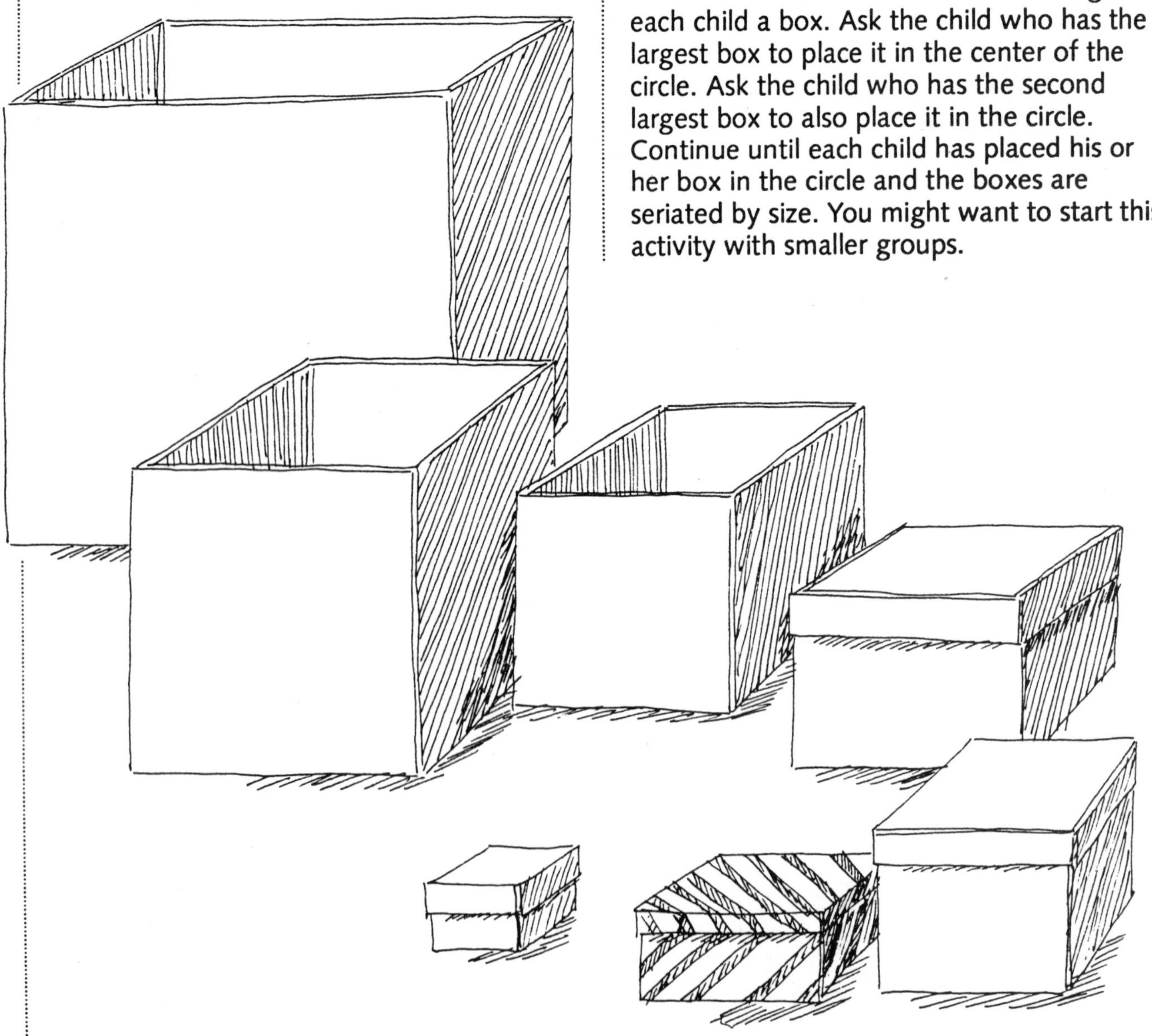

Listen and Count

✔ Metal box, marbles

Invite children to close their eyes as you drop marbles, one by one, into a metal box. Have children count the number of marbles dropped. Invite children to take turns dropping the marbles in the box.

Match the Shape

✔ Assorted boxes and containers, cardboard, felt markers

Divide the class into three groups. On large pieces of cardboard cut from boxes, trace a geometric shape (circle, square, rectangle) and give one to each group. Pile an assortment of boxes and containers on the floor. Challenge each group to find all the boxes and containers that match the shape outlined on their piece of cardboard.

Nesting News

✔ Assorted boxes, colorful adhesive-backed paper

Select several boxes that can be nested one inside the other. Remove the lids and cover with colorful adhesive-backed paper. Invite children to fit the boxes inside each other.

Stack 'Em High

✔ Assorted boxes, notepaper, pencils

Pile a large collection of boxes on the floor. Invite students to predict the number of boxes they can stack. Have children write the number on a piece of paper. Challenge students to stack the boxes until one falls and then compare the number in the stack with the prediction.

Same or Different?

✔ Assorted boxes

Invite each child to select two boxes from the collection and tell how the boxes are alike and how they are different.

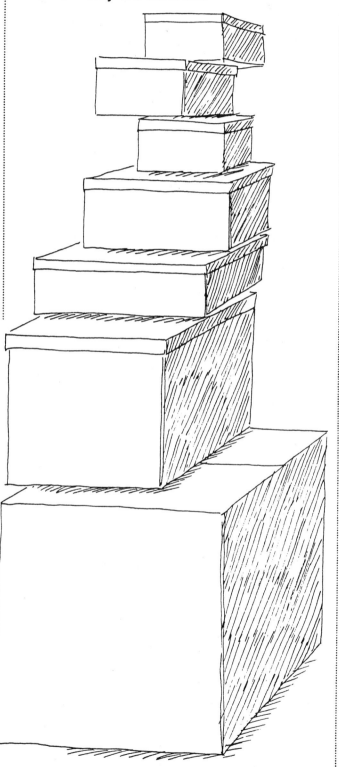

Chapter 17 Art with Boxes and Cartons

Boxes and cartons of all sizes can be cut, painted, and decorated by young children to create a vast number of interesting and useful projects.

Hanging Art

Tree Decorations

✔ Small boxes, gift wrap, ribbon, tape

Invite children to wrap small boxes in gift wrap and tie them with a ribbon. Add an extra loop of ribbon to make a hanger to hang the gift-wrap ornament on a tree.

Learning Tree

✔ Small boxes, paint, bare branch, plaster of Paris, pot, ribbon

Place a bare branch in a pot of plaster of Paris and allow the plaster to harden. Invite children to paint small boxes in different colors. Attach like-colored ribbon loops and hang the boxes on the tree branch. Use the hanging colored boxes for color recognition games. For example, ask children to gather all the red boxes or hang the blue boxes on the right side of the tree. Invite children to make boxes with shapes, numbers, children's names, or new words to hang on the tree. Use the boxes for more "Learning Tree" games.

Mobiles

✔ Small boxes, paint, hole punch, string, wire hanger, scissors

Invite children to paint small boxes. Punch a hole in each box, attach string in different lengths, and hang the boxes from a wire coat hanger. Challenge older students to remove one side of the box and paint a picture inside before hanging the boxes as a mobile.

Picture Frame

✔ Shirt boxes, scissors, picture or painting, glue

Invite children to cut a large window from the lid or bottom of a shirt box to create a frame. Children can glue a picture or painting they have made inside the box behind the frame. Hang the framed artwork around the classroom.

Decorated Boxes

Keepsake Box

✔ Boxes, collage materials (beads, sequins, dried flowers, glitter, yarn, macaroni, beans), glue

Give each child a box with a hinged or removable lid. Invite children to decorate their boxes with collage materials. Suggest that students use the boxes to keep their special treasures.

Collection Box

✔ Shoe boxes, glue, fabric and wallpaper scraps, colored tissue paper

Invite each child to decorate a shoe box by gluing fabric and wallpaper scraps or colored tissue paper on its sides. Have children brush a mixture of equal parts of glue and water over the entire collage to give it a glossy look. Encourage students to use the boxes to start their own unique collections.

Sculptures

Building with Boxes

✔ Boxes, scissors, glue, paint, construction paper

Give each group of children a piece of cardboard, cut from a box, to use as a base. Invite groups to work cooperatively to build creative box sculptures by gluing an assortment of boxes to the base. Encourage students to paint their sculptures or add details made with construction paper.

Box Animals

✔ Assorted small boxes, glue, felt markers, paint

Invite children to glue small boxes together to form animals. Children can paint the animals and add facial features using felt markers. Invite children to make barns from boxes to house their animals.

Box Cities

Houses

✔ Large appliance boxes, scissors, paint

Invite students to help create houses out of large appliance boxes placed lengthwise or upright. Cut squares and rectangles around three sides to make doors and windows with hinges. Encourage children to paint the houses. Invite children to create an entire neighborhood by adding stores, a school, street signs, and house numbers.

Neighborhood

✔ Small boxes, large box, scissors, paint, glue

Invite each child to make a house from a small box. Encourage children to cut out doors and windows and paint their houses. Cut a piece of cardboard from a large box to use as a base. Invite children to glue their houses to the base to create a neighborhood. Children can paint streets, grass, and trees as well.

Shopping Mall

✔ Small boxes, large box, scissors, paint, glue

Invite each child to make a store from a small box. Encourage children to cut out doors and windows and paint their stores' names on the fronts of the buildings. Cut a piece of cardboard from a large box to use as a base. Invite children to glue their stores to the base to create a shopping mall.

Gas Station

✔ Large boxes, small boxes, scissors, paint

Invite students to cut several doors and windows in a large box to make a garage. Glue the garage to a cardboard base cut from another larger box. Invite children to create gas pumps from upright toothpaste boxes and cars and trucks from other smaller boxes. Encourage children to paint roads on the cardboard base as well.

Doll Play

Dollhouses

✔ Large boxes, small boxes, scissors, collage materials, paint, felt markers

To make a one-story house, tip a box on its side so the open end faces front. To add additional rooms, tape boxes side by side. Cut doors and windows and encourage children to make furniture and decorations. To make a two-story house, tape boxes on top with the open ends facing front.

Doll Furniture

✔ Small boxes, scissors, paint, glue, fabric or wallpaper

Invite children to remove the lid from a small box and paint it to make a doll bed. Children can invert a small box (lid removed) to make a table. Invite children to cut out portions from each side of the inverted box to make table legs. Invite children to glue small boxes to the backs and sides of flat boxes to make chairs and sofas. Children can cover the furniture with fabric or wallpaper.

Rocking Doll Cradle

✔ Oatmeal boxes, scissors, tape, fabric or wallpaper, paint

Cut a section from a large oatmeal box from the top to the bottom. Replace the lid and tape in place. Invite children to paint or cover the rocking cradle with fabric or wallpaper.

Doll Clothes Closet

✔ Shoe boxes, scissors, adhesive-backed paper, wooden dowels, glue

Remove the lid from a shoe box and cover the outside of the box with adhesive-backed paper. Stand the box on its end. Cut a hole on each side of the box near the top. Slide a wooden dowel through the holes and glue in place.

TV Fun

Live TV

✔ Large appliance box, scissors, paint

Cut a large window in an appliance box. Invite children to paint knobs and a control panel on the front. Encourage students to be newscasters, sports announcers, weather forecasters, comedians, and singing stars. Give students time to prepare their scripts. Encourage students to take turns standing inside the TV and making presentations.

TV Scroll

✔ Large appliance box, scissors, long cardboard tubes, butcher paper, felt markers, magazines, glue

Cut out a large window in an appliance box. Cut holes on both sides of the screen at the top and the bottom. Push a cardboard tube through both pairs of holes from side to side. Invite children to draw or glue pictures from magazines on a long sheet of butcher paper. Roll the paper on the tubes inside the box, taping one end of the paper to each cardboard tube. Place the box on the floor so the screen is facing up. Invite children to turn the tubes to roll and unroll the pictures. Children can make mini-versions of this TV using shoe boxes and wooden dowels.

Puppets

Wand Puppets

✔ Small boxes, heavy cardboard, scissors, felt markers, yarn, paint, construction paper, glue, sequins, fake fur

Give each child a 2" x 12" cardboard strip. Invite children to decorate a box to look like a puppet head and glue it to the top of the cardboard strip. Encourage children to hold the wand to manipulate the puppet.

Finger Puppets

✔ Small boxes, tape, scissors, paint, felt markers, yarn, construction paper, glue, sequins, fake fur

Have each child tape a lid shut on a small box. Cut a hole in one end of each box so that a child's finger will fit inside. Encourage children to decorate the box to look like a puppet.

Bouncing Puppets

✔ Small boxes, string, rubber bands, stapler, paint, construction paper, glue, felt markers, sequins

Invite children to attach small boxes together with strings to form jointed people or animals. Invite children to decorate the boxes and add facial features. Cut a large rubber band and staple one end to the top of the puppet head.

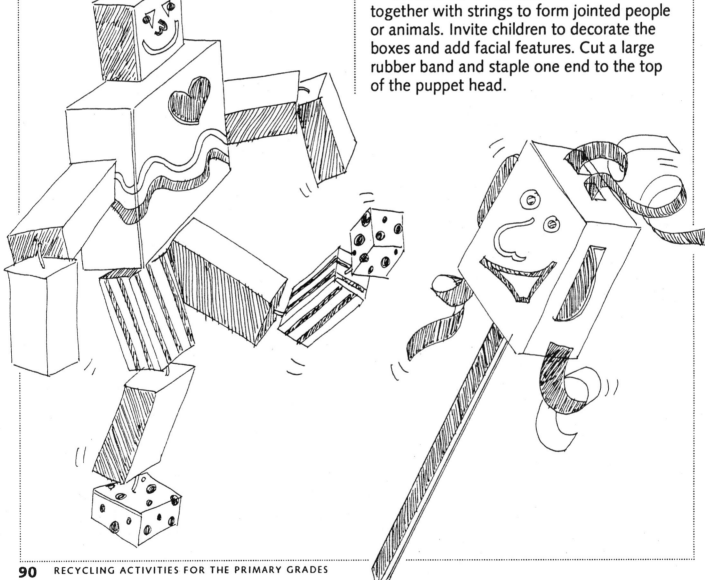

Marionettes

✔ Small boxes, string, rubber bands, stapler, paint, construction paper, glue, felt markers, sequins, heavy thread, scissors, hole punch

Invite children to attach small boxes together with strings to form jointed people or animals. Invite children to decorate the boxes and add facial features. Cut five lengths of heavy thread. Attach a piece of thread to the top of the head and to each puppet hand and foot. Cut a 6" x 3" strip of heavy cardboard for a control board. Punch one hole in a 3" side and two holes on each 6" side. Have children tie the other ends of the strings to the holes in the control board. Tie the head thread to the hole on the 3" side, a hand to each of the two front side holes, and a leg to each of the two back holes. Invite children to hold the control board in one hand and manipulate the strings with the other.

Puppet Stage

✔ Box, scissors, felt markers, paint

Remove the lid from a box and cut a large window in the box bottom. Invite children to decorate the box. Place the box on a table so the window faces the audience. Children can operate puppets from behind the window. To make a lap stage, use a smaller box. Invite children to hold the box on their laps and operate finger puppets from behind the window.

Games

Box Puzzle

✔ Cereal boxes, scissors, small boxes

Cut the front picture from a cereal box. Invite children to cut the picture into puzzle pieces. Store the puzzles in individual boxes.

Game Dice

✔ Cube-shaped boxes, tape, white adhesive-backed paper, paint

Tape the lid shut and cover a cube-shaped box with white adhesive-backed paper. Paint large dots on each side (one through six). Encourage children to use the large dice to create their own games.

Chapter 18 Dramatic Play with Boxes and Cartons

Children can let their imaginations flow as they transform boxes and cartons into costumes and other accessories for dramatic play.

Costumes

Shape Suit

✔ Large boxes, tape, scissors, hole punch, yarn, paint, construction paper, glue

Have children cut both ends from a box big enough to fit over their bodies. Encourage children to paint, or cut from construction paper, geometric shapes in different colors. Have children glue the shapes on their boxes. Help children punch two holes in the front at the top of the boxes and two in the back. Help children place the boxes over their heads. Tie double strands of yarn through the holes to make shoulder straps. The top of the box should fit just below the child's arms. Children can make a clown suit using a similar box and decorating it appropriately.

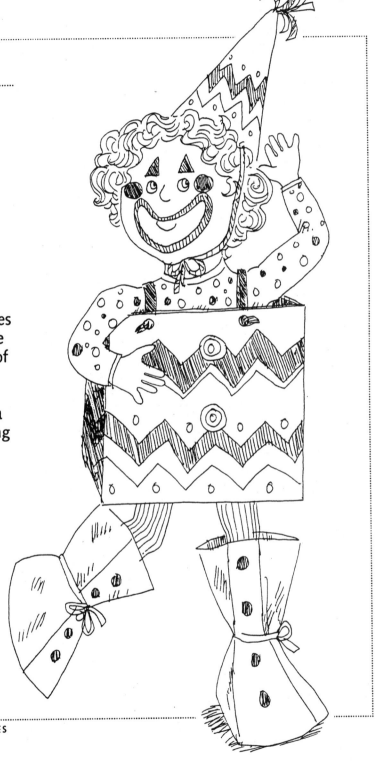

Space Attire

✔ Large boxes, scissors, paint, silver glitter, felt markers, glue, five-gallon ice-cream cartons

Help children cut out one end of a box and then cut a large head hole in the opposite end. Help children mark and cut armholes in the box. Invite children to paint and decorate their boxes. Children can make a space helmet by cutting a window from one side of a five-gallon ice-cream carton (with lid removed). Encourage children to paint and decorate their helmets.

Signboard Suit

✔ Large boxes, hole punch, yarn, scissors, paint, felt markers

Help each child cut two large, rectangular pieces of cardboard from a large box. Punch two holes in the top of each cardboard piece. Have children tie yarn through the holes to connect the two pieces and make shoulder straps. Encourage children to paint and decorate their signboard suits.

Hats and Masks

Tall Hats

✔ Oatmeal boxes, paint, hole punch, yarn, glitter, scissors

Invite each child to paint an oatmeal box to make a tall hat of their choice. For example, students can paint the container black to make a stovepipe hat or gold to make a bandleader's hat. Encourage students to decorate their hats by adding yarn pom-poms, tassels, or glitter. Help children punch a hole on opposite sides of the open ends of their hats. Tie lengths of yarn through each hole so students can tie the yarn under their chins.

Valentine Hat

✔ Heart-shaped candy box, hole punch, yarn, construction paper, glue, scissors

Invite students to decorate a heart-shaped candy box. Help students punch a hole on opposite sides of the box and attach yarn to tie under their chins.

Holiday Hats

✔ Boxes or five-gallon ice-cream containers, scissors, holiday decorations (lace, flowers, Easter grass), glue, hole punch, yarn

Help children cut circles from cardboard or use the lids from five-gallon ice-cream containers. Invite each child to decorate a circle to make a holiday hat. Encourage creativity and inventiveness. Punch a hole on opposite sides of the hat and attach yarn to tie under the chin.

Round Lid Mask

✔ Boxes or five-gallon ice-cream cartons, scissors, colored plastic wrap, tape, hole punch, wide rubber bands, paint, decorating materials

Give each child a lid from a five-gallon ice-cream carton or a round cardboard circle cut from a box. Cut appropriately placed eyeholes in each circle. Invite children to tape colored plastic wrap to the backside of each eyehole. Encourage children to decorate their masks. Help children punch a hole on opposite sides of the circle. Cut and tie a wide rubber band through the holes to fit the mask around the child's head.

Accessories

Dangling Belt

✔ Small boxes, yarn, hole punch, felt markers, paint

Invite each child to punch a hole in several boxes and tie a length of yarn through each hole. Have children tie the boxes to a piece of yarn long enough to go around their waists. Encourage children to decorate the boxes using paint or felt markers.

Necklace

✔ Small boxes, yarn, hole punch, felt markers, paint

Invite each child to punch a hole in several boxes and tie a length of yarn through each hole. Have children tie the boxes to a piece of yarn long enough to make a loose necklace. Encourage children to decorate the boxes using paint or felt markers.

Pendant

✔ Small boxes, yarn, hole punch, felt markers, paint, magazines, glue

Invite each child to string a single box on a length of yarn to make a pendant necklace. Invite children to decorate the pendant by gluing on a picture from a magazine or a photograph.

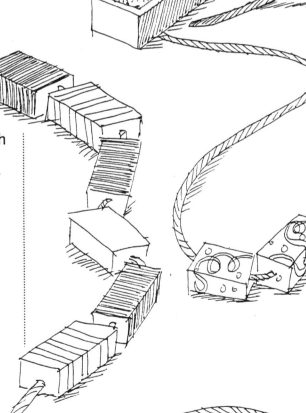